This collection of about 100 poems by Lal Singh Dil (1943-2007), a Punjabi revolutionary poet, represents a distinctive voice in the Punjabi poetry inspired by the Naxalite (Maoist) movement in the early seventies of the 20th century. Belonging to a 'low caste' tanner community, Lal Singh Dil grew up facing isolation, indignities and insults heaped upon the 'low castes'. He joined the Naxalite movement hoping that the revolution would bring about social and economic equality, liberating him, and millions like him, from the curse of social exclusion and economic deprivation. But the revolution never happened, the movement died down, and he lived and died excluded and marginalized.

Apart from singing of the revolution, its hopes and defeat, these poems bring out the nothingness of the lives of the low caste landless labourers and daily wagers, and nomads of all varieties, moving from place to place like animals foraging for food, toiling in others' fields for almost nothing, grazing their cattle, gathering animal dung, performing so many tasks reserved for the 'menials' in the traditional Indian socio-economic system.

About the translator

T C Ghai (b.1937) has taught English language and literature at Deshbandhu Evening College (now Ramanujan College), University of Delhi. He has published two short novels, *The Stricken Moth* (1984) and *Alone in the Wilderness* (2000), both from Writers Workshop, Kolkata; poems in the *Journal of the Poetry Society (India)* and also done poetry reviews (1991-94) for the same journal. He has translated two Punjabi poets into English, Dr Puran Singh Kanwar (*A Season of Nights*, 2006) and Avatar Singh Sandhu Pash (*Pash: A Poet of Impossible Dreams*, 2010); and short stories of the Hindi fiction writer Premchand, which are available on his blog INTERACTIONS at http://ghai-tc.blogspot.in/

Exclusion, Deprivation and Nothingness

Lal Singh Dil

Selected Poems

Translated from Punjabi
by **T C Ghai**

First Published 2017

ISBN 978-93-83723-27-0

Published by
LG PUBLISHERS DISTRIBUTORS
49, Lane No. 14, Pratap Nagar
Mayur Vihar Phase I, Delhi 110 091
Tel : 011 2279 5641 email: lgpdist@gmail.com

Typeset at
Arpit Printographers, Delhi

Printed at
Mudrak, Delhi

Contents

FROM **SUTLEJ DI HAWA / BREEZE FROM THE SUTLEJ (1971)**

FROM **BAHUT SAAREY SURAJ/SO MANY SUNS (1982)**

FROM **SATTHAR /A SHEAF** **(1997)**

EXTRACTS FROM **AJJ BILLA PHIR AAYA / BILLA CAME AGAIN TODAY (2009)**

Introduction

Lal Singh Dil: His Life and Poetry

Lal Singh Dil (1943-2007) was one of the leading revolutionary poets emerging out of the *Naxalite* (Maoist-Leninist) movement in Punjab towards the late sixties of the last century. The other prominent poets belonging to this group were: Avatar Singh Sandhu Pash (1950-1988), Amarjit Chandan (1946-) and Sant Ram Udasi (1939-1986). Although the movement in Punjab was a political failure and died down quickly, it led to radical changes in the subject matter, language and idiom, tone and tenor of Punjabi poetry. Lal Singh Dil's contribution to these changes has been very distinctive. He has focused for the first time in Punjabi poetry on the lives of people excluded and ignored by history and disinherited from the fruits of civilization, progress and development for ages — men and women belonging to the wandering tribes of Punjab (*Sansi, Bauaria, Bazigar, Barad, Bangala, Gadhile, Nut* etc.), the landless labourers and daily wagers mostly belonging to the lower-caste communities. Another very important impact of the emergence of Dil, and Sant Ram Udasi (who also belonged to a lower-caste community), has been the rise of many writers among the 'excluded' castes who are now writing for the first time in Punjabi frankly and boldly about the humiliation they and their communities have faced and continue to face at the hands of the upper castes.

His Life

1943-72

Lal Singh Dil was born on 11 April in 1943 in a Ramdasia

'chamar', (a lower-caste community of tanners) family in Ghungrali Sikhãn, a village near Samrala, a small town in the Malwa region of Punjab. His was a family without money, without land, without education, without any financial and intellectual resources that could give Lal Singh a start for upward social and economic mobility. The family was fitted to perform only manual and menial agricultural labour, and Lal Singh's father, Ronki Ram, almost throughout his life, worked as an agricultural labourer on someone's land. The family, like most of the Ramadasia community in the Malwa region of Punjab, subscribed to Sikhism, yet there is hardly any record in Lal Singh's poetry or his autobiography that he or his family seriously practised any aspect of their religion.

Lal Singh Dil passed high school examination from Government School Samrala in 1960-61, being the first in his family to pass tenth standard and go to college. He joined A.S. College at another town, Khanna, close by, but dropped out after one year. He joined Junior Teachers' Training course in 1964 at SHS College in Bahilolpur, another close-by town, but gave up after two years without completing the course. He spent a year studying for Gyani, an honours course in Punjabi Literature, but did not complete the course. During this period Lal Singh supported himself by working as a wage labourer and herder, and by giving tuitions.

Right from his childhood he was constantly reminded that he belonged to a 'lower caste'. This is what he writes in the opening paragraph of his autobiography, *'Dastaan'*: 'I have endured the ordeal by fire time and again in my life, and it is a miracle that I have been able to emerge unscathed.' (Dil 1998, p. 13) What that fire was he illustrates with an example in the next few lines of the same opening paragraph. While as a small boy of five or six, out of innocence, he dares to bathe at a Jat farmer's well. He is immediately dragged away, whip-lashed thrice and, driven out by the farmer's son. As a 'chamar' he is not permitted to bathe at the well of an upper caste. He is pushed into this 'fire' again and again; at school where he is stopped from playing a small part in a play, or never considered for a 'cleanliness' award; at college where he dares to fall in love with an upper caste girl and becomes the object of ridicule; and later even within the egalitarian Naxalite movement and the poetic fraternity. 'There is caste even in poetry. Everyone keeps talking about Pash because he is a Jat. No one reads Lal Singh Dil,' complained Dil.

Lal Singh is said to have been introduced to Marxist ideology when he was at college. Although no details are available of his initiation, he was already a determined revolutionary when the Naxalite movement arrived in 1967. This is how he himself describes his enthusiasm for the Naxalite movement: 'The news of Naxalbari spread like wildfire. Those days I was working as a labourer on daily wages. I carried heavy loads up and down a ladder, and all this activity gave me strange energy. I felt now I would be able to accomplish what I could have achieved had I been present during the upsurge in Vietnam. I felt I was on the threshold of realizing the imminent Revolution.' (Dutt 2012, p. 53) He took part in a Naxalite agitation (Birla Seed Farm Agitation, Ropar) in 1969 and later, in the same year, was member of an amateurish group of Naxalites who unsuccessfully raided the police station in the town of Chamkaur on 30 April 1969. He, like others, fled from the scene but was soon arrested and subjected to severe police torture during a long period of police custody, specially becoming a target of the Hindu upper caste and Sikh Jat police officials. He was tried and sentenced to 'six months imprisonment with hard labour' (Dil 1998, p. 115), in his own words. He remained in jail sometime between of 1969 and 1971. After release from jail in 1971, fearing police persecution, facing neglect from family, friends and comrades, and lacking moral or financial support from any quarter he fled to Uttar Pradesh.

1972-83

In Uttar Pradesh he moved from one town or village to another, seeking one or another kind of subsistence employment about which he talks extensively in his autobiography. His friend, Prem Parkash, Punjabi short-story writer, says: 'I received one letter from Lakhim Kheri. It was evident from his letters, many of which are lost, that sometimes he worked with the Imam in a mosque, and sometimes he was caretaker of a factory, sometimes he looked after orchards, sometimes he turned a cloth vendor moving from village to village. He also lived in a timber godown.' (Parkash 1998, p. 171) Sometime in 1972 he had converted to Islam. His arguments for conversion make very interesting reading:

> The next day a thought occurred to me. We shall be able to establish a new culture only after we have brought about a revolution. Why shouldn't I, until that time, adopt one from the existing cultures? I was impressed by the way these people (the Muslim family he happened to be working with) related to one another and also by the attitude of the villagers. It took me no time to come to the conclusion that a person who can't be a Muslim can never be a communist. Which means, I believed that Islamic culture was nearest to the communist culture. The only difference being that the former was theist and the latter atheist. I thought I should accept Islam until the communist culture became a reality, but still remaining an atheist. This was a strange thought. That I should adopt Islam, and at the same time remain a non-believer! (Dil 1998, pp. 129-30)

This is what Dil wrote to his friend Amarjit Chandan in 1973:

> First of all let me tell you that I have become a Musalmaan. I have been circumcised and have learnt to say the namaz. I have also acquired the requisite knowledge. This is not accidental. Even before this I had my heart in Islam and only my intellect in communism. Since I was a non-believer, both my heart and intellect were dedicated to communism. (Chandan 1998, p. 9)

This conversion, however, did not go down well with his Marxist friends back at home who were shocked to hear a fellow communist turn an apostate. It took them time to accept Dil's conversion. Amarjit Chandan writes, 'He fondly remembers the days spent in UP. He had reached the place of which Bulleh Shah had dreamed of. There no one knew his caste, and neither did anyone believe in caste... Inspired by this atmosphere and also in the hope of finding a female companion he one day converted to Islam... After publishing his letter in *'HemJyoti'* I had written that Lal Singh was dead. I now greatly regret that folly. I hope the *dervish* has forgiven me...' (Chandan 1998, 2007, pp. 26-27)

In his Afterword to *'Dastaan'* Prem Parkash writes, '....from his letters it appears that his wounded heart and soul has at last found solace now. He has found refuge in a great power. Here not only his body but all his basic rights as a human being have become secure.' (Parkash 1998, p. 171)

It seems Dil had resolved the conflict between his heart and intellect at least for the time being, and become a believer and a devout Muslim. In one of his letters to Prem Parkash, he wrote: 'Mao's name should be struck out where ever it occurs in my poetry. It was *kufr* (apostasy). And whatever I have written against God be burnt.' (Ibid., p. 172) Dil, however, did not succeed in finding a female companion even in Islam.

In Uttar Pradesh he did not give up writing poetry. He was in contact with Urdu poets of the region and wrote many *Naats* and Ghazals in Urdu, but he continued to write in Punjabi. 'Between 1972 and 1983, I came into contact with Urdu poets of the town Mohammadi,' (Dil 2006, p. 30) writes Dil. While here, in Uttar Pradesh, he wrote his poems published as *'Bahut Saarey Suraj'* (So Many Suns) (1982).

1983-2007

He returned to his home town Samrala sometime in 1983, but no one welcomed him; neither his family, nor his friends, nor the poetic fraternity. Unable to find any support or vocation he left for Gujarat to work on someone's farm on subsistence wages and stayed their till 1985. Back in Samrala again, he could not find any regular employment or source of income. Prem Parkash in his Afterword writes, 'There was a time when Lal was completely idle. He had no contact with any literary person, nor anyone in his neighbourhood. He would go and sit in the crematorium in the company of a *baba*. Whatever food the *baba* brought he shared with Dil and a bitch and its litter. Dil used to discuss Sufism with the *baba* and consume Lord Shiv's drink, bhang. He had also begun to fantasize about women. For a considerable period he was fantasizing about Amrita Pritam.Later when Nirupama started enticing him away from his tea stall to Nilo's bridge by offering him beer and cigarettes, he transferred his thoughts on to her... For some time he fantasized about a female political leader too.' (Parkash 1998, pp. 173-74)

He did receive some financial support from a few friends and well-wishers. He was also helped to set up a tea stall, which he ran, on and off and without success, for about two years at the bus terminal close to his hometown, Samrala, dispensing tea to truck drivers among others. Like a devout Muslim he continued to say his daily namaz, but also remained addicted to drinking. He even acted as a maulvi for some time in the town mosque and taught children to read Urdu or say the namaz. His inability to properly support himself or his addiction to drinking led to many a discord between him and his brothers. He renewed his contacts with the literary world, attending poetry symposiums, or reciting his poems on All India Radio and Doordarshan, Jalandhar, and also continued writing poetry under his old name. Penury, drinking and neglect and perhaps also an unstable state of mind took their toll and his health progressively deteriorated. He died on 14 August in 2007 in a hospital in Ludhiana. This is what Satya Pal Sehgal of Panjab University Chandigarh, who has recently translated Dil's poetry into Hindi, has to report on the last days of Dil:

> On the afternoon of 10 August 2007, when I and Dr. Sukhdev Singh reached his residence, the home of his brothers, at Samrala in District Ludhiana, we saw that the oppressively hot and humid room in the upper floor, on which he (Dil) was lying on his deathbed, was unfit even for animals to live in. Everything in the room was covered in dust. The sagging cot, bricks lying here and there, an old dust-laden box, some tattered old books, some trinkets and a few shields covered with cobwebs. There was no window, except for a small hole in the wall made by removing a few bricks, and even this hole was partly blocked with a piece of ragged cloth. A mere skeleton, Dil was lying on the cot, limp and

almost lifeless. It was clear that he was near his end. He was taken to a hospital in Ludhiana where he died on 14 August... And worst of all, no one took seriously, or showed any consideration or sensitivity, before and after his death, towards his conversion to Islam to escape his life-long curse, and cremated him according to the traditional Sikh rituals. *In the end, he could make no dent at all in his Dalit Sikh destiny.* In the meanwhile, on their way to the cremation ground, comrades were raising slogans: *Dil, we shall keep your dream alive, with determination!* (Sehgal 2013, p. 13)

His Poetry

Lal Singh Dil had started writing poetry even while at school. Some of his poems were published in well-known Punjabi magazines, *'Lakeer'*, *'Preetlari'*, even before his first collection of poetry was published. He published three collections of poetry: *'Sutlej Di Hawa'* (Breeze from the Sutlej) 1971; *'Bahut Saarey Suraj'* (So Many Suns) 1982; and *'Satthar'* (A Sheaf) 1997. A collected volume of all his published poems titled *'Naglok'* (The World of the Serpent People) and his autobiography, *'Dastaan'* were published in 1998. He also wrote a long poem titled *'Ajj Billa Phir Aaya'* (Billa Came Again Today), which was published in 2009, posthumously. A collection of three of his verse plays (Kav Natak), *'Rano Gitan Wali'* (Rano, the Songstress), *'Parwane'* (The Moths), and *'Dukhi Ram'* (Unhappy Ram), was published in 2012.

Although he had converted to Islam and adopted Muslim names (Muhammad Bushra and Wali Mohammad), he had continued to write under his pre-conversion name. He also wrote many poems in Urdu, mostly in praise of the Prophet or on similar themes, but they were not published, and it is not known where the manuscripts have gone.

How to enter into Dil's poetic world? A person living in a metropolis and outside Punjab, in a big city, would have to travel a long distance on a lonely, narrow and deserted road cutting through wilderness and pre modern landscapes, leaving behind all the prominently visible symbols of wealth, modernity, urbanization, industrialization and progress – the cities, the glittering malls, the high-rise buildings, the television, computers, mobile phones, the gigantic airliners, and even the now less modern images of modernity like the textile mills, overhead telephone and power lines, trains and buses. One might as well have moved almost into Premchand's rural India, if not the 19th century rural India.

The modern urban world, as well as the world of wealth or even minimal affluence, is almost completely absent from Dil's poetry, as also from his imagination. His poetry delineates mostly the lives of people for whom modernity and urban life are non-existent, or almost irrelevant, even as a dream. For most of them, life revolves around agricultural land, which does not belong to them but to which they are tied down by chains of servitude for subsistence and survival. For them life does not mean much beyond this. Most of them belong to the landless dalit and many wandering tribal communities mostly invisible in the mainstream media, and until recently in history and literature.

Added to this, one must also keep in mind the intellectual background out of which his poetry emerged. Dil, it seems, was not a great reader of books. He just did not have the means to buy or access many books or other written materials. Most of his reading, apart from whatever little he had read at school and college, I believe was confined to books and magazines in the Punjabi language. It won't be very wrong to say that his understanding of life, of history, religion and society, and even of the communist ideology, was mostly picked up from his surroundings, from the popular culture, so to say. This makes his poetry distinctive and different, for it has a quality of the raw, the unformed, the folk and the mythic. His poetry gives voice to the voiceless, the ignored, and in their language, through their unsophisticated mixture of truth and belief, prejudice and superstition, anger, bitterness and humour, desire for revenge, and for transcendence as in fairy tales.

Dil's poetry is primarily the poetry of experience of subaltern communities, of an imagination embedded in popular culture and folklore, trying ceaselessly to excavate experiences of sub human existence that had been the fate of his subjects throughout much of history. To be able to enter into that world and clearly listen to these voices one must shed all pre-conceived bourgeois notions of what is good art or good poetry and realize that presentation of experience in the raw may transcend any such aesthetic considerations. In Dil's poetry art, the constructed image of reality, and presentation of life in the raw as lived by people outside the pale seem to work side by side.

Dil's first three collections of poetry, later published collectively as *'Naglok' (1998, 2007)*, form a corpus that can be clubbed and studied together because they were published in his life time, and together form a kind of unit that can be set apart from *'Ajj Billa Phir Aaya'* (Billa Came Again Today), which was published in 2009 two years after his death. Moreover, *'Ajj Billa Phir Aaya'* along with Dil's *'Kav Natak'*, three verse plays, published in 2012, reveal Dil's understanding of the dalit question in a new context, and more fully and somewhat differently.

Naglok (1998)

The title *'Naglok'* seems to link the people who inhabit Dil's poetic world with the cult of serpent worshippers, the pre-Aryan inhabitants of India, and also the mythical people, *Nagas*, inhabiting the *'Patal'* (the underworld) in the Punjabi folk cosmology, and the Puranic *'Patal' or 'Nag-Lok'*, both idealized and heavenly regions. (See 25 under Notes)

The poems in the first collection, *'Sutlej Di Hawa'* (Breeze from the Sutlej) *(1971)*, were mostly written during the peak of the Naxalite movement in Punjab. Most of the poems in this collection reflect the rise of the revolutionary movement, its elan, its arrogance, and its hope of imminent success by overthrowing the existing system; a hope that was short-lived and proved illusory. Here in one poem, *My Country*, the poet identifies himself with all the oppressed people within the country and the world at large, and imagines a world without borders.

It won't be wrong if one said that the first two poems in this collection, *'Breeze from the Sutlej'* and *'The Colour of the*

Evening' define the thematic range of Dil's poetry from the beginning to the end. They confront us with three basic concerns of Dil's poetry: the people who have been the victims of socio-economic oppression and injustice since ages; the roots of that oppression in history; the revolutionary awakening among these people to overthrow this repressive and unjust socio-economic and political system, and establish an egalitarian society. And Dil sets up a binary opposition between 'Aryan' and 'Dravidian' which gradually unfolds itself with great force in his poetic career over time.

Caste discrimination looks to take a back seat in this collection. The Marxist-Leninist revolutionary ideology subsumes caste under class. The awareness of caste discrimination, however, is not absent. But in this collection it finds expression primarily as personal experience in his love poems (*'On Diwali Night'*, *'Love's Self Murder'*, *'Caste'* and *'A Thought'*) in which one can feel the pain of rejection because of caste.

One might say that under the influence of Marxist ideology Dil is yet unable to fully express the deadly stranglehold of caste in the Indian society. In this very first collection one can already see in operation Dil's skill in constructing short poems, which remained his chief strength as a poet. *'Nadeen'* and *'The Outcasts'* are very fine examples of this.

'Kangla Teli'

Dil's longish narrative poem in this collection, *'Kangla Teli'*, creates a new type of hero in Punjabi literature, a rebel from a lower caste who knits together a coalition of the lower castes against an oppressive king.

'Kangla Teli' may be subsumed under the well-known genre of narratives called fairy tales in which human beings of humble origins are transformed into heroes or heroines. Stories that come to mind immediately are, *'The Brave Little Tailor'*, *'Jack the Giant Killer'*, *'Cinderella'* and *'The Brave Potter'*. In all these tales an ordinary and a lowly born, a neglected child, or a physically weak and timid person is transformed into a hero who slays

many giants and dangerous animals, defeats armies, inherits or wins a kingdom and marries a princess, or a prince as in the case of Cinderella. None of these characters are endowed with great physical or mental powers. Their success is mostly the result of either good luck or chance combined with trickery and common sense, often aided by magical powers conferred on them by some supernatural agency. All these stories can be called, in Freudian terms, stories of wish-fulfillment, 'the wish to make another world that is not real'. To put it simply, we achieve in dreams or in our fantasies or in stories we invent what is not possible in real life.

On the face of it, Dil's *'Kangla Teli'* looks similar to these fairy tales, but there are differences. The hero here may be of lowly origin, but he is a brave and daring young man — 'brave as a lion'. Kangla's victory over Bhoj is not secured with the help of any supernatural power or by chance but through a well-planned and recognized strategy, a *guerilla* assault. It is a conscious daring act, and also an act of revenge. However Kangla's triumph remains incomplete. For, unlike other fairy tales, the story does not end happily. His wife, Rehmatan, to save her honour, kills herself before the king can seduce her; this act, though, turns her into a worthy heroine. His father, Peerudit, dies of a shock the moment he hears of Rehmatan's abduction. And, Kangla remains a partially realized hero. People are not sure how Raja Bhoj was killed. Was he eaten up by a lion, or killed by Kangla? They just can't believe that Kangla could match Raja Bhoj in status and physical strength, much less kill him.

Although Dil's story may not fully conform to the conventional fairy tale typology, the underlying motive is similar. It is essentially a fantasy of the poet's mind, the realization of his revolutionary aspirations. Dil perhaps sees himself in the role of Kangla Teli, a revolutionary hero. Another probable explanation for Dil's creation of a rebellious character in Kangla might be the prevalence of such characters in the myths, legends and history of Punjab and the Punjabi people's admiration for them. I am referring to rebels like Dulla Bhatti, Raja Rasalu, Guga Pir, Banda Singh Bahadur, Jagga Daku, and

Udham Singh and Bhagat Singh. Dil in this poem has created a folk hero from a lowly caste.

In the next collection, *'Bahut Saarey Suraj'* (So Many Suns) (1982), one can see a change. The poems in this collection were mostly written during his exile in Uttar Pradesh, perhaps between 1972 and 1978 and chart a different kind of experience. The number of revolutionary poems is small and there is nothing of hope or elan or optimism in them. They delineate a mood of wishful thinking. Obviously the revolution has become a distant if not an impossible dream, as in the poem *'The Wave'*.

The focus in this collection now shifts on the depiction of people's lives, their misery, their struggles and sufferings, their humiliations, their deprivations, their helplessness, as also their defiance, and even joy and celebration in the face of all these. Who are these people? This is what Sarabjit Singh writes about the people who inhabit Dil's poetic world:

> They are people without land, without religion, without culture, and considered barbaric by the established social order, and deprived of their humanity. They form a group of the disinherited from all angles. (Singh 2006, p. 60)

The awareness of caste now takes a different turn in poems that go back to the past to explore the roots of discrimination in history. The Aryan-Dravidian opposition now looms larger in many short and long poems. Especially the poem *'Kudeli Pind Dian Wasna'* (The Women of Kudeli Village), is an expression of a highly self-conscious social outcast's complete alienation from the Hindu (or Aryan or Brahmanical) civilizational superstructure. The women of Kudeli consciously align themselves with what is regarded as dark, evil, villainous and dangerous in the mainstream worldview: Ravana, Rakshasas, thieves and the most venomous snakes. The poem is a telling illustration of how in Lal Singh Dil's poetry an utterly uncompromising dissent sometimes operates as a silent and subterranean but powerful undercurrent. In just a few lines Dil so skilfully and effortlessly turns the mainstream Hindu worldview upside down and what is evil becomes good and what is good becomes evil. It is one of Dil's most remarkable poems, both for its intensity, brevity and superbly crafted form.

One of the poems in this collection, *'Falian To Tikhe Dand'* (Teeth Sharper than Ploughshares), introduces a theme that assumes far bigger importance in his long poem *'Ajj Billa Phir Aaya'* (Billa Came Again Today), where the big landowning Jats, the zamindars, who have 'grabbed' most of the land, have replaced the conquering 'Aryans' as the arch oppressors.

The poem *'Uchchi Niwin Sabhyata'* (Culture High and Low) seems to portray a Utopia that, Dil believes, was lost by the aboriginal inhabitants of India, somehow related to the *nagas*, the serpent people, inhabiting the *naglok* or patala, the seventh and the lowest region of the Puranic underworld, through the Aryan conquest.

His third collection, *'Satthar' (A* Sheaf*) (1997)*, contains poems mostly written after his return from UP, between 1983 and 1997. This collection, containing 64 poems, is disparate both in terms of the subject matter and quality. A number of poems don't come off and show a decline in poetic vigour, which might be the result of his declining mental and physical state. It still contains a number of revolutionary poems but the tone has altogether changed. He seems to have lost the hope of any change, and his poems about the revolution express his dismay and disillusionment. His tone about the revolutionaries is one of derision, and which hardly conceals the poet's bitterness.

The other poems continue to portray the people of Dil's world—the people just at the margins of everything. These are people who are acted upon, are passive recipients of abuse of all kinds, getting support from nowhere. The state as godfather is nowhere visible; yet the state and society as oppressors are present everywhere.

Some of his poems go back to his experience in UP. A few have Islamic colour. Some of the poems delineate his personal experiences, as a chowkidar and a tea-vendor, and a few of them focus on women. The overall impression is one of poetic decline, yet many poems still display the poet's old fire and take on deeply symbolic meanings. Particularly poems like *'The Bull'* and *'Tea Shop'*. If the former delineates the sapping of the revolutionary urge in terms of a castrated bull, the latter seems to sum up Dil's whole life. The revolutionary hope is no doubt dead but the desire is still alive, and for Dil the only hope of escape for his people still lies in a revolution.

Billa Came Again Today (2009)

'Ajj Billa Phir Aaya' (Billa Came Again Today), running into a little over a hundred pages was most probably written between 2004 and 2006 when Dil was mentally unstable and economically down and out.The poem is a first person narration, somewhat similar to a journal, and the focus of the poem is the fate of the dalits of Punjab. It is a narration of the poet's encounter with his own self, with his town Samrala through a person called Billa and a few other characters in the story.

The poem opens with a statement that the poet is in the grips of a fear creeping through his heart like a snake, and all he can do to overcome it is to write a poem. This is followed by a narration of a number of dreams and nightmares that are bizarre and surrealist, and gradually the cause of the fear unfolds itself. It is the Green Revolution that has played havoc with the lives of the dalits. His own town Samrala, has become the city of the unemployed and under-employed youth who have become drug addicts and are dying in large numbers.

Having drawn an image of the dalits and his town Samrala and explained the immediate cause of their plight, the poet then turns to the reader to show him the roots of dalit repression in history through Aryan conquest and enslavement of Dravidians, the aboriginal inhabitants of India. The poem ends on a note of uncertainty, posing the question as to how to tame this monster called the Green Revolution that has swallowed everything good and worthwhile.

> Finally, how shall we deal
> with this monster?
> He has devoured everything ...

For all its flaws, which are many, the poem is a very remarkable achievement considering the circumstances under which it was written. It is a poem in prose, a narrative with many passages of beautiful poetry, and frightening and gory nightmares, a montage of literary genres. There is an element of great detachment, serenity, and little trace of rancor or anger or self-pity. One might say that in this long poem Dil breaks new ground and goes beyond *'Naglok'* to explore far more elaborately the depths of dalit repression in terms of, what Dil believes, was a total falsification of history by the conquering Aryans.

His Verse Plays (2012)

The plays, written towards the end of his life, and published posthumously in 2012, add a new dimension to Dil's view of the dalit question.

The first two plays are very short. The first one, *'Rano Gitan Wali'* (Rano, the Songstress), shows the communists in a positive light. The second play, *'Parwane'* (The Moths), valorizes a long line of martyrs from Banda Singh Bahadur through the Ghadarites to Bhagat Singh and comrade Bujha Singh. The plays are devoid of real merit but they show the primary sources of Dil's inspiration, the communist ideology and the Sikh tradition of martyrdom that still remain part of his ideological repertoire and revolutionary hope.

The third play, *'Dukhi Ram'* (Unhappy Ram), is longer and interesting because it brings to surface very forcefully the concerns at the heart of Dil's poetry. This play, a fast moving dramatization of the Ramayana in rhyming couplets has no real literary merit. But it is an attempt to appropriate Rama as a Dravidian prince. Here Sita's banishment by Rama is shown to have been forced upon him by the brahmanical Rajguru, which he later regrets; and the incident of the shudhra ascetic Shambuk's beheading by Rama is excluded from the story. Thus Rama is absolved of the two most unforgivable deeds; both, for Dil, Aryan interpolations to malign a Dravidian prince.

Finally, how to make sense of this subaltern maverick poet's journey from '*Sutlej Di Hawa*' (1971), his first collection of poetry, to his last publications '*Ajj Billa Phir Aaya*' (2009) and his '*Kav Natak*' (2012); of his journey from almost a pure and simple Naxalite revolutionary (placing all his faith in Marxist-Leninist revolution to transform not only his life as an individual but also the whole world), through his conversion to Islam, and finally to reclaiming for Dalits, the descendants of the 'Dravidians', the aboriginal inhabitants of India, the space forcibly occupied by their arch tormentors, the 'Aryans'. The last two works and the last few years seem to show a strange contradiction. His physical world has shrunk and become limited to his home town Samrala and his community. It excludes the rest of the world. More strangely it excludes almost everything that happened in Punjab and India between 1983, when he returned from UP, and his death in 2007.

But if his physical world has shrunk, his intellectual and spiritual world seems to have expanded and become more inclusive and more complex, if not more chaotic. His sponge-like mind seems to have absorbed so many things. The dream or the illusion of a communist revolution still remains at the heart of his thinking. But it has got mixed up with many other things. He continued to practice some kind of Islam, saying namaz like a devout Muslim, yet did not stop drinking. He has also drawn from the long tradition of martyrdom beginning with the Sikh Gurus and continuing to the present day through the Ghadarites and Bhagat Singh. His hostility to what he believes is 'Aryan' remains as strong as ever. May be it has become stronger. But at the same time he has counter-appropriated for 'Dravidians'(and dalits) much that he once believed to be 'Aryan', which includes Rama and the Vedas, though after divesting them of what he believes to be their brahmanical impurities! He has also appropriated '*Guru Granth Sahib*' as a dalit *Granth* because it contains the *vani* of Guru Ravi Das, asserting that Sikhism has also fallen prey to the 'Aryan' perfidy. All the blame for repression, injustice and discrimination is thrown on the 'Aryan' civilization, or Brahmanvad, which now functions through zamindars in alliance with other upper castes and leaders of his own community and through elections.

What to make of this unusual mindscape? Is it a messy cocktail comprising a half-digested political ideology, elements from diverse religions and belief systems, folklore and popular history, myth and invention born of a life-long neglect, anger and pain? Or, a schizophrenic mind's oscillations from one extreme to another, a mind that is desperately looking for and unable to find a resting place? Or is it an inclusiveness comprehending three millennia's conflicting and conflating, clashing, overlapping and coexisting world views, medley of belief systems and folk practices for which Punjab and north-west were perhaps the first battleground in the Indian sub-continent?

Farid Shakarganj (1173/88–1266/80), the 'first' Punjabi poet, has become immortal for just 112 couplets (Slokas) of poetry, not merely because these verses were made a part of the Sikh scripture by the fifth Guru of the Sikhs but also because Farid had become entrenched in the minds and hearts of a large mass of people across all the Punjabi-speaking communities in much of the Northwest of the Indian subcontinent for giving expression to something fundamental in human experience—the transience of life and the existentialist pain of living.

Dil's poetic achievement is also very significant. He has brought to the forefront of Punjabi poetry the lives of people who had so far been confined beyond the pale of history and even memory. He has produced a sizable body of work that for its subject matter, its emphasis and also its quality and an extreme sensitiveness to pain, both personal and of those like him, remains very distinctive. This achievement combined with some accident of fortune might immortalize him too. He did reveal that too human a desire, when he told Ajay Bhardwaj, when he was filming him for his documentary, *'Kitte Mil Ve Mahi'* (Where the Twain shall Meet): *'chote bira tain minu amar kar ditta'* (Younger brother, you have made me immortal). (Bhardwaj 2012) And this is what Dil said once to Prem Parkash while they stood in his ramshackle courtyard in Samrala: 'After my death, build my shrine here. And hold a fair every year, with the singing of qawwalis.' (Parkash 2006, p. 126)

So, why not celebrate him, and bring him one step closer!

T C Ghai

REFERENCES

Bhardwaj, Ajay. 2012. The idea shift behind 'Kitte Mil Ve Mahi' (Where the Twain Shall Meet). Excerpts from field notes on the making of 'Kite Mil Vet Mahi'. Available at: http://ajaybhardwaj.in/films/the-idea-shift-behind-kitte-mil-ve-mahi/

Chandan, Amarjit. 1998. Adhurey Safar Di Poori Dastaan (Complete Story of an Incomplete Journey). In Dil, Lal Singh. *Dastaan: Svai Jeevani* (Dastaan: An Autobiography) (Ludhiana: Chetna Parkashan) pp. 5-12

Chandan, Amarjit. 1998, 2007. Bahut Chupp Kitiyan Da Kavi (A Poet of Understatement). In Dil, Lal Singh. *Naglok* (Ludhiana: Chetna Parkashan) pp. 23-30

Chandan, Amarjit. 1998, 2007. Sampadaki (Introduction) Bahut Sarrey Suraj (So Many Suns). In Dil, Lal Singh. *Naglok* (Ludhiana: Chetna Parkashan), pp. 98-100.

Dil, Lal Singh. 1998, 2007. *Naglok* (Ludhiana: Chetna Parkashan)

Dil, Lal Singh. 1998. *Dastaan: Svai Jeevani* (Dastaan: An Autobiography) (Ludhiana: Chetna Parkashan)

Dil, Lal Singh. 2006. Mera Urdu Mahol (My Urdu Environment). In Tarsem S (Dr.) (Ed.). *Lal Singh Dil: Sankalap Te Smikhkya* (Lal Singh Dil: A Critical Appreciation) (Chandigarh: Lokgeet Parkashan) pp. 30-31

Dil, Lal Singh. 2009. *Ajj Billa Phir Aaya* (Billa Come Again Today) (Chandigarh: Lokgeet Parkashan)

Dutt, Nirupama (tr.). 2012. *Poet of the Revolution: The Memoirs and Poems of Lal Singh Dil* (New Delhi: Penguin Viking)

Parkash, Prem. 1998. Udno Bachaye Warke (Pages Salvaged from being Blown Away). In Dil, Lal Singh. *Dastaan: Svai Jeevani* (Dastaan: An Autobiography) (Ludhiana: Chetna Parkashan) pp.170-175

Parkash, Prem. 2006. Makbarey Da Pir: Lal Singh Dil (The Pir of a Mausoleum: Lal Singh Dil). In Parkash, Prem. In *Umran Di Khatti* (A Life-time's Earnings) (Chandigarh: Lokgeet Parkashan) pp. 125-135

Sehgal, Satyapal (Dr.) (tr.). 2013. *Lal Singh Dil: Pratinidhi Kavitayein* (Lal Singh Dil: Representative Poems) (Panchkoola: Aadhar

Prakashan) pp. 11-18

Singh, Sarabjit (Dr.). 2006. Pathrayi Manukhta Da Parvakta (Spokesman for the Stone-dumb Mankind). In Tarsem S (Dr.) (Ed.). *Lal Singh Dil: Sankalap Te Smikhkya* (Lal Singh Dil: A Critical Appreciation) (Chandigarh: Lokgeet Parkashan) pp. 56-67

Note: *All translations from the Punjabi language sources are by the translator unless otherwise stated.*

Lal Singh Dil's Poetry: A Discourse of Dissent

Reading Lal Singh Dil's poetry raises many bitter and distasteful questions in one's mind. But the question that troubles the most is whether human beings like him do really live on this earth. If they do, which part of the world do they inhabit?Poet Lal Singh Dil does not belong to the world by which we swear; he is an inhabitant of an altogether different world. He has turned his back on us and shares nothing with our so-called civilized world. He not only outrightly rejects the dominant, unequal socio-economic and brahmanical dispensation that has reduced people like him to objects of contumely and debasement, his rebellious spirit does not even recognize as valid the long established and commonly accepted truths, traditions, belief systems, moral and aesthetic values and myths. Dissent is the central tenet that drives his awareness of life and his creative expression. His poetry redefines the concepts like nation, race, man, religion, morality, culture and aesthetics:

My country has yet another name
I have yet another kinship:
Where there's even one street
half hungry
half asleep
where drudgery
counts the stars
to comfort its aching limbs:
Wherever it is

away from my homeland
it is my own country, my own brotherhood.

– from *'Desh'* (My Country) in *Sutlej Di Hawa* (Breeze from the Sutlej)

The hungry and the naked, 'the other', of whose life Dil's poetry is an authentic portrayal, do not belong to a different star but are the original inhabitants of this land. History has been unjust to them. This 'other Bharat', living in makeshift 'bamboo huts', transporting their babies in 'cauldrons' and roaming on 'donkey backs' in search of livelihoods, inhabited this land long before the advent of Aryans. The women who are now termed 'Adivasi' were once 'queens'. The people who wander from place to place burdened with the belief that they were born from the feet of a god were once the masters of this land. The victorious Aryans have so camouflaged this truth that they have turned the natives of this land into aliens in their own home. The forcible denial of the means of material life to them makes the very idea of nation, race, and even history, questionable. For the dispossessed these concepts no longer remain objects of pride, rather they smack of treacherous conspiracies. Histories of the socially dominant classes become the means of enslaving the weak and the helpless. In this regard Lal Singh Dil's poetry becomes a scathing commentary on the myth of racial and national pride and the authenticity and function of history. The terms race, nation and history no longer retain a neutral meaning, rather they become carriers of the ideological bias of the powerful. In Dil's poetry these categories have been interpreted from the point of view of 'the other', because Dil believes that the chasm between 'you and us' can neither be measured nor bridged. One of his characters says:

This isn't the distance between Earth and Mars
that rockets can measure
Nor the distance
between Delhi and Moscow or Washington
that you measure everyday

The distance
between you and us
is such
as only arrows can measure

– from *'Doori'* (The Distance) in *Sutlej Di Hawa*
(Breeze from the Sutlej)

The dalit world, of whose tragic existence Dil's poetry is a heart-rending portrayal, is the victim of a double-edged deadly curse: economic inequality, and the humiliating Manuvadi social exclusion. Facing physical and psychological repression for centuries, facing degradation even to fulfill his minimal daily needs, the trampled-down dalit begins to doubt his own humanity. His very existence seems to him a cruel joke. His consciousness, stunned by this dual shock, turns him into stone or a dumb animal. Constant mental torture, physical violence and demeaning struggle for left-overs fill his body and soul with lassitude. A consciousness turned to stone remains unmoved even if 'the beloved is crushed under a wheel', or 'the brother goes mad', or 'the mother is disrobed by the police'. A mind 'wriggling like a trapped worm' sees nothing as his own. In spite of being part of a country, a community, a religion, a culture, the individual feels alienated. His existence becomes a burden for him and he becomes an outsider even in his own home:

Dogs bark:
'My home! My home!'
The landlord:
'My village! My kingdom!'
The leader:
'My country! My country!'
People :
'Our fate! Our fate!'
What should I say?
This weariness!
This state of inaction!

My brother? My friend? My daughter? My mother? My country?
Nothing is mine.

– from *'Thakewan'* (Weariness) in *Bahut Sarrey Suraj* (So Many Suns)

Lal Singh Dil's poetry portrays the lives of dalit men and women who are broken-down, ignorant and who feel shame-faced at their own existence and have become aliens in their own home. At the centre of his poetry are the people who have been deprived of everything, and who have been turned into 'chandals' by power politics and the Manuvadi varna dispensation. So much so that even their own lips are unable to express their pain. Dil's poetry presents an altogether new image of the animal-like existence of the silently suffering yet potentially rebellious people. Winnowers rambling from door to door, humiliated donkey drovers, wayfaring snake charmers, ironsmiths awake whole nights in their huts, nomadic blacksmiths, wage labourers walking to work with tear-filled eyes, hired farm workers pleading for a few mouthfuls of food, landless peasants forced to sell even the whey, grass-cutters in soiled clothes, naked and barefoot herders, innocent girls carrying heavy dung-filled baskets, naked small girls picking berries, brides decked in old clothes, and adorned with cheap creams and soaps, female labourers bearing with the foul language of landowners, mothers collecting firewood from trees forced to alight, women labourers wearing black like rakshasas, and socially excluded prostitutes – such are the people who inhabit his poetic world. We find many authentic images of people who are at the lowest rungs of Indian society and have been completely dehumanized. That is why Dil has called the people of his poetic world *'Naglok'* – the world of the ignored, the invisible insect-like people. As examples one may read poems like *'Shaam Da Rung'* (The Colour of the Evening), in *'Sutlej Di Hawa'* (Breeze from the Sutlej); *'Machchiwada'*, *'Kum to Pichchon'* (After the Day's Labour), *'Kudeli Pind Diyan Wasana'* (The Women of Kudeli Village), *'Bholiyan'* (The Innocents),

'Adivasana' (Tribal Women), and *'Weswa Trimtan'* (Prostitutes) in *'Bahut Sarrey Suraj'* (So Many Suns); and *'Lal Poorav'* (The Red East), *'Ghode Charan Waliye Kudiye'* (The Girl Tending Horses):

Once again the grain winnowers walk off
an alien land.
A long train of people is on the move
carrying loads of insults
casting long shadows
children riding the donkeys
fathers holding their dogs
mothers carrying cauldrons
on their backs
with their babies asleep inside.
A long train of people is on the move
carrying on their shoulders the poles for their huts.

Who are these hunger-driven Aryans!
Whose land in Bharat
are they now planning to grab!

– from *'Shaam Da Rung'* (The Colour of the Evening) in *Sutlej Di Hawa* (Breeze from the Sutlej)

Habitations where, in the red dust,
hungry, tender-bodied girls are seen
carrying heavy baskets.
Habitations where bare-footed mothers
walk away for the day's labour.

Habitations where the weaver
plying his loom the whole night
collapses into sleep at dawn
as if a heavy wheel in a mill
should suddenly break down
leaving his children crying for the morning meal.

Habitations where blacksmiths
keep awake the whole night

their lives burning out with their lamps.

Habitations where peasants
feed on humiliation
having to sell off even the whey.

– from *'Lal Poorav'* (The Red East) in *Sutlej Di Hawa* (Breeze from the Sutlej)

If this story were ever told
to the inhabitants of another star
they would turn into stone
and never wake up
Were the animals to sense this
they would flee to the jungles
shrieking, in fright of mankind

– from *'Bholiyan'* (The Innocents) in *Bahut Saarey Suraj* (So Many Suns)

Lal Singh Dil expands the geographical space of Punjabi poetry. The progressive poetry before him also delineates the tragic lives of peasants and workers, but the people whom he brings to the centre of his poetry (blacksmiths, cattle drovers, winnowers, snake charmers and the tribal people), although not strangers, have been outsiders for us. The range of Punjabi poetry before him remained circumscribed to the delineation of the lives of peasants and wage labourers working on agricultural land in the villages, and the middle classes living in cities. The village and the city are only half visible in that poetry. Dil's poetry brings us face to face with subaltern people who exist beyond the world familiar to us and whose dehumanized existence sends a shiver through our spines. Not only is the image of man presented in his poetry a new one, his vision of human existence is also different. He does not look at the people (subalterns) pushed by the powerful to the margins and forced to live like animals, as objects of pity or subjects for romantic treatment. Neither do we find in his poetry the fire and thunder of his contemporary Naxalite poets. He is not a poet pouring out, like boiling lava, the anger of the victims of economic and social exclusion but one who gives expression to their anger in a subdued yet telling voice. Dr. Gurbachan is right when he says: 'Lal Singh Dil's poetry talks of the marginalized and the weak, yet it is the mainstream that is the target. ('*Who are these hunger-driven Aryans?*') He sets out to describe the winnowers and women wearing black, yet the axe falls on the Indian culture and the green fields.' (*Kis Kis Tarah De Sikandar* [So Many Alexanders], p. 189). When Lal Singh Dil portrays the plurality and uniqueness of many disappearing and neglected aspects of Indian culture, he expands the definition of words like nation, race, region and culture; and our faith in the humanity of the down-trodden and repressed groups – dalits, nomadic people, women and Adivasis – begins to revive. In this manner his poetry negates the process of dehumanization of the destitute and voiceless:

It's Punjab everywhere:
all around
villages surrounded by trees.
The appearance hardly distinguishable
veiled under bundles of grass
a dirty towel
an unkempt beard
the shirt black with sweat and dust
bare legs
cracked heels.
Whether in Bengal
or in Kerala
the herdsmen, driving their cattle
through a haze of dust,
look like Punjabis.

— from '*Punjab*' in *Bahut Saarey Suraj*
(So Many Suns)

The tribal women come,
they pull and pluck fruits.
They have their babies in their laps.

They say:
We were queens
We married off our servants
among the forest folk
These bounties
were given away by our men.

– from *'Adivasnan'* (Tribal Women) in *Bahut Saarey Suraj* (So Many Suns)

The worst victim of economic disparity and Manuvadi caste system is the woman. In our male dominated patriarchal society, the fate of the subaltern/dalit female is even worse. The image of the female in Lal Singh Dil's poetry is far different from her image in our subconscious. It conforms neither to the sensually attractive image present in our erotic literature, nor to that of the fearless Durga who can protect herself and the weak; nor is it that of the self-conscious and assertive woman of the progressive poetry who has the capability to understand the complexities of the present unjust order and confront it. The image of woman in Dil's *'Naglok'* is that of one who is innocent, naïve, and defeated; who helplessly accepts the repressive dispensation as her destiny. The life of this woman humiliated in her deprivation is full of thorns. Such women, labouring for others, are neither Mohinis nor Manekas nor Munishas – they are Adivasi women wearing 'black' and doing 'black' deeds. The women in Dil's world are not the ones respected and loved in our homes and society as daughters, sisters, wives and mothers, but disrobed prostitutes. To have a glimpse of the world of Dil's women one may read poems such as *'Beganian'* (The Outcasts), *'Chhal'* (Insurgence), *'Kudeli Pind Diyan Wasana'* (The Women of Kudeli Village), *'Bholiyan'* (The Innocents), *'Adivasanan'* (Tribal Women), *'Weswa Trimatan'* (Prostitutes), and *'Ghode Chardiye Kudiye'* (To the Girl Tending Horses). These poems, full of passionate expression, do not evoke any pleasurable feelings, rather they make us shame-faced:

Cleaning up the mangers
gathering cow-dung
or wheat spikes:
They work very hard
these gentle outcast daughters.
Spiky straw, hot plates,
sharp-edged vegetable cutters,
needles—
as if all these had been trained
to hurt their hands and feet.

– from *'Beganian'* (The Outcasts) in *Sutlej Di Hawa* (Breeze from the Sutlej)

The women of Kudeli, wearing black,
pass through the gardens green
to labour in the fields.
They know Ravana's people wore black
even then they wear black.
They know the demons wore black
even then they wear black.
They know the thieves wear black
even then they wear black.

– from *'Kudeli Pind Diyan Wasanan'* (The Women of Kudeli Village) in *Bahut Saarey Suraj* (So Many Suns)

Near naked innocent girls
picking berries
gathering leaves of milkweed
broken pieces of pottery
making mud chapattis
counting the dresses for their doll
dresses as old and ragged as their own
wrapping berries in milkweed leaves
all to be displayed as dowry for their doll

– from *'Bholiyan'* (The Innocents) in *Bahut Saarey Suraj* (So Many Suns)

That is why perhaps Dr Harbhajan Singh calls Dil's poetry the poetry of 'panchang swaras' (five musical notes) which, by breaking the brahmanic myths, challenges the mentality built upon the varana dharam. In his words: 'These poems don't give us joy, they shame us. The poems that give us pleasure work to stabilize the already established values. The shaming poems uproot a person from his fixed position and challenge him to renew himself. ... Lal Singh weaves his subtle satire through the images of innocent girls. If you want to know how forceful innocence can be, listen to Lal Singh Dil'. ('*Naksh Nawerey*' [New Footprints] from Introduction to *Bahut Saarey Suraj*) (So Many Suns) (1982)

Lal Singh Dil, through the subtle play of his satire and tone of dissent, rejects our established ideas of beauty and femininity. He overturns the feudal image of woman as a weakling and an object of sensual pleasure. How far can the notions of beauty and erotic pleasure be relevant in the dalit's embittered and envenomed world filled with deprivations? There is no place in Dil's poetic world for the sensually playful female heroines. His heroines are: 'a labourer woman baking her heart on a *tawa*'; a woman guerrilla fighting till the barrel of her gun melts; the dark complexioned woman who 'throws into fire' all the taboos and restraints of feminine modesty; Nammah's wife who strips herself naked to dance; and the ostracized prostitute. Dil's poetry mocks at the traditional image of a modest and docile female. In our society the woman who violates the established moral code is characterized as a 'bastard' or a prostitute. She is not our sister or daughter and cannot be a member of our morally correct society. When Lal Singh Dil calls the prostitutes as his own and the revolution's sisters and daughters, he hits out at the hypocritical upholders of morality who, in fact, themselves disrobe unsuspecting and innocent females. By challenging the traditional view of the female as an object of pleasure or as an image of modesty, Dil opens up a path for the return and acceptance into the society of the female who has been banished by the male dominated politics and society. In this way Dil's poetry not only questions the prevalent models of femininity but also expands and creates other parallel models of femininity:

> When
> that dark complexioned woman
> in an overflow of joy
> says: I'm a bastard out and out
> she hurls so many things,
> like me,
> into the fire pit under the coal tar drum:
> images
> books
> the roof under her feet
> and
> brickbats brickbats brickbats.

– from *'Chhal'* (Insurgence) in *Bahut Saarey Suraj* (So Many Suns)

> These prostitutes
> are my mothers, sisters and daughters
> and yours too
> and they are mothers, sisters and daughters
> of the cow-worshipping India
> and they are mothers, sisters and daughters
> of Bharat, the worshipper of non-violence and the Buddha
> and they are mothers, sisters and daughters
> of the big capitalists.
> If not
> then they are mothers, sisters and daughters
> of the imminent revolution.

– from *'Weswa Trimantan'* (Prostitutes) in *Bahut Saarey Suraj* (So Many Suns)

The people who have appropriated the means of production in the society have not only deprived peasants and workers of the material comforts and conveniences but also invented myths characterizing them as uncivilized and animal-like, as chandals, idlers, rakshasas, thieves, lustful, paupers and shirkers. In the politics of power the down-trodden can be kept enslaved only by crushing their self-respect and humanity. Dil, who has had a bitter taste of it, understands this. For a 'chamar' boy to write poetry, to fall in love with a girl of a higher caste, to dream of social justice through a revolution – was not only sinful but also very risky. Lal Singh Dil took this risk with a conscious understanding. During the Naxalite movement he suffered greater persecution from the police because being 'a low caste' poet he had dared to talk of a revolution to transform the society. He was mentally broken down by the caste-ist conduct of his upper caste girl friend's mother, and also of the members of the Naxalite groups. As a reaction he ran away to Uttar Pradesh and changed his religion. His body and soul were crushed by the police beatings and humiliating comments on his low caste status, yet his poetry did not lose its fire. He did not let the edge of his words become blunt. Dil knows quite well that the liberation of the lower castes is not possible until the social values and ideological hegemony of the classes owning the means of production are destroyed. The poems like *'Bhumia Daku'* (Bhumia, the Dacoit), *'Kangla Teli'*, *'Nammah'* and *'Ajooba'* (A Wonder) overturn the myth of the workers and women being weak and helpless:

> People say the earth rests on a bull's horns.
> I don't agree.
> I am firm
> that woman carries the earth
> in her hands.
> That's why the earth smells of a woman's body
> That's why the crops wave like women's scarves...
> The earth and woman share the same pain.

– from *'Ajooba'* (A Wonder) in *Bahut Saarey Suraj* (So Many Suns)

During the peak of the Naxalite movement (in Punjab) Lal Singh Dil wrote poetry that supported the use of counter-violence. Like other poets of the revolutionary movement he too approved of the use of counter-violence to seek liberation from repression. In his poems like *'Sutlej Di Hawa'* (Breeze from the Sutlej), *'Rihai Di Khushi Vich Geet'* (A Song to Celebrate Release), *'Belachak'* (Inflexible), *'Kangla Teli'*, *'Lal Poorav'* (The Red East) and *'Uthan Guerrilley'* (Let Guerrillas Rise) he pleads for a politics of armed guerrilla warfare and revenge. That the repression by the powerful can be ended only through counter-violence was the central tenet of the revolutionary poetry of those times. That the dignity and self-respect of the physically and mentally repressed can only be restored through counter-violence was Lal Singh Dil's understanding too during the seventies of the last century. That is why one of his characters says:

> They want to throw us
> upon the green wavy reed grass
> or among the fragrant hill-kikar trees.
> We shall drag them under our feet
> into the drains
> into dung heaps
> like dogs.

– from *'Belachak'* (Inflexible) in *Sutlej Di Hawa* (Breeze from the Sutlej)

This rage, however, is not the characteristic note of Dil's poetry; his achievement lies in creating a low-key note of satiric understatement. His satiric language at once shakes the reader accustomed to the traditional aesthetic criteria and established value systems. Along with the established values he also rejects the bourgeois poetic and aesthetic theories. He characterizes as leprosy-stricken the established principles about life and art, as also the books; and even their scholar-interpreters who, he says have sold out their vision and conscience. He rejects the bourgeois art criteria because they prolong the life of the established values. In poems like *'Naach'* (The Dance) in *Sutlej Di Hawa* (Breeze from the Sutlej), and *'Kavita'* (All is Poetry) in *Bahut Saarey Suraj* (So Many Suns) he presents an alternative image of art and aesthetics. According to him the art of the simple people absorbed in their daily toil is plain, unpretentious, spontaneous and outspoken. A challenging-questioning posture, instead of the sly and obsequious one, is the hallmark of the working class art. The face burnished with hard labour has its own beauty. Dil's poetry presents without romanticizing the beauty of the toiling working classes with their sun-scorched faces, discoloured dresses, and unrecognizable faces hidden under heavy loads. For him the very rhythm of a toiler's life is living art:

> When the labourer's wife
> bakes her heart on a tawa
> the moon smiles through the *shisham* tree.
> The father drums the empty bowl
> to humour his younger son.
> The elder one dances, and
> sets jingling the tiny bells girding his waist.
> Then, it seems
> neither the song
> nor the dance
> can ever end.

– from '*Naach*' (The Dance) in *Sutlej Di Hawa* (Breeze from the Sutlej)

Lal Singh Dil's poetry challenges, along with the traditional life styles, the established aesthetic standards and poetic practices. According to him, 'the words awake at all times like a mother are worthy of being called poetry'. His own poetry has played this role successfully.

(*Translatd from Punjabi*)

Sukhdev Singh
Professor
Department of Punjabi
Panjab University Chandigarh

On Translating Dil

Lal Singh Dil is the third Punjabi poet I am translating. Before him I had translated my colleague Dr. Puran Singh Kanwar's (1942-1996) collection *'Rattan Di Rutt'* (characterized by a critic as 'poetry of a unique paradigm in Punjabi') as 'A *Season of Nights'* (National Bookshop, Delhi, 2006) and the fiery revolutionary poet Avatar Singh Sandhu Pash's (1950-1988) 100 poems as *'Pash: A Poet of Impossible Dreams'* (Shilalekh, Delhi, 2010).

The present collection contains about 100 poems of another revolutionary poet, Lal Singh Dil, selected from *'Naglok'* (Chetna Parkashan, Ludhiana, 2007), a collection of his three works of poetry published between 1971 and 1997, and a few extracts from his long poem *'Ajj Billa Phir Aaya'* (Billa Came Again Today) published in 2009 after his death. *'Naglok'* contains about 135 five poems and *'Ajj Billa Phir Aaya'* is about a hundred pages long; admittedly a small corpus, but path-breaking in Punjabi poetry. The poems I have selected are fairly representative, and would reveal the heart and soul of Dil's poetry very substantially.

I had become familiar with Lal Singh Dil's poetry while translating Pash, his contemporary Naxalite poet, and was intrigued by the sad fact that a poet should have to sell tea (and wash used tea cups) for a living. The desire to know more about this person had taken hold of me and made me delve deeply into his life and poetry. Reading him, especially his autobiography, *'Dastaan'* proved truly revealing. Autobiographies are supposed to be 'spectacular' in many ways. They may be confessionary, or driven by a desire for self-expression, self-glorification, fame, money etc. Dil's autobiography is spectacular for the very absence of such aspirations.On the contrary it showcases what it means for a person to be treated almost as the last dreg of a society, to be utterly marginalized: It is exclusion from almost everything that civilization provides for its fortunate children that Lal Singh's story preeminently highlights. Yet Lal Singh writes with great dignity, without cringing and with his head held high. It is this that makes *'Dastaan'* spectacular. And his poetry? It is a narrative of the wretched of the earth told by one of them. A few things stand out and make his poetry worth reading, talking about and sharing: That such a man dared to dream of a revolution; that he pursued the vocation of a poet in all circumstances to write about the most marginalized people; that he remained an outcast and a rebel.

I had started working on translating Dil sometime in 2011.I was supported in this by my friend Prof. Ronki Ram of Panjab University. I was further pushed into it by a well-known Punjabi poet, Amarjit Chandan, also a contemporary of Lal Singh in the Naxalite movement, now settled in UK, whom I 'met' fortuitously on the Internet. He suggested that I should send some of Dil's poems for publication in the translation magazine MPT (Modern Poetry in Translation) founded, by Ted Hughes and Daniel Weissbort in 1965, published from Oxford, UK. The magazine publishes translations of poetry, past and contemporary, from languages all over the world. As a result five of Dil's poems were published in that magazine in 2012, which gave Dil a bit of international exposure. Later I also put Lal Singh Dil on the Wikipedia. It would please readers of Dil's poetry to know that MPT has included two of Dil's poems out of these in their golden jubilee anthology, *Centres of Cataclysm, 2016,* which is a selection from a few thousand poems published in MPT since 1965.

About the actual translations, I don't claim to fully understand Dil's poetry. So there might be a few howlers which the Punjabi readers of Dil would be able to recognize, and may forgive. Dictionaries have not always been helpful because many turns of phrase in Dil's colloquial language (Malwai, the Punjabi dialect spoken in the Malwa region of Punjab) seldom find a place there. However, I offer no excuses and hope there are not too many howlers. It is also quite natural that some readers may not feel satisfied with my reading and understanding of Dil's poetry. I know that my translations are just one of the many imperfect ones that are possible. I have made no attempt to reduce Dil's by and large plain and straight forward free, sometimes prosaic, verse into any English poetic mould and make Dil speak like an English poet. My translations are closer to the literal, line by line and even word for word, and may at times violate the natural rhythm of English. They do not capture the flavour, the sounds and rhythm of idiomatic Punjabi, miss many nuances of Punjabi life and culture, and may understate the context of the bleak lives Dil's poetry portrays. On occasions in Dil's poetry the line between art and life seems to disappear, and may give the reader the impression of lack of poetic rigour where content seems to overthrow form. The readers should understand that Dil's poetry is primarily the poetry of experience, of a person entrenched in popular culture and folklore. As I have already said, in Dil's poetry art, the constructed image of reality, and presentation of life in the raw as lived by people outside the pale seem to work side by side. However I hope readers would be able to recognize Dil's fine craftsmanship in many of his shorter poems. I shall be more than satisfied if my translations are able to capture both the art and artlessness of Dil's poetry, and convey the deprivation and humiliation, anger and defiance, hope and frustration, the emptiness, the pain and suffering that characterize the lives of Dil's people and of which his poetry is a testimony.

Finally, why did I translate Dil into English? We all know that English language in India through translations is evolving into a confluent site for so many disparate voices from scores of Indian languages and dialects, enriching itself enlarging its perspective, giving itself a real flavour of India's rain-forest diversity, which is only minimally reflected in the Indian English Poetry. Such translations of regional and vernacular poetry into

English enable readers to hear voices that not only surprise, delight and expand their awareness but also shock and disturb and bring within their earshot what is unheard or willfully ignored, or contemptuously dismissed as too commonplace. Dil's poetry, I believe, makes us hear one such voice that questions, rejects, overturns and subverts many traditional and mainstream notions of state, nationalism, religion, art, culture and society.

T C Ghai
New Delhi

FROM SUTLEJ DI HAWA / BREEZE FROM THE SUTLEJ

(1971)

Breeze from the Sutlej

I

When I saw you wafting through
the reed-grass fields
I fell in love with you.
I found you in my breath,
I found you in my arms.
The stink from the Raj Bhawans
could not touch your pure soul
because you rise from the waves
that had once enfolded
in their wounded hearts
the martyrs[1] hanged in Lahore.
Here, each morn
each night, each day, each evening
is mournful.
Songs arise here
as herder boys
on their cattle's backs
wade through the waters.
I see you lost in sadness.
Your billowing currents
become my sails
towards islands of daring.
I saw you in the trees
in the listless wheat fields
in the fragrance of *Kikar*[2] trees.
You can see
right up to the Kaveri

lands being grabbed
the wheat crops being insulted
the smiling paddy fields being scorched.
You can see
sprawling far and wide, the Raj Bhawans
that still wield even today
the white man's noose.

II

This sadness of yours won my heart
and I saw you in the shape of a beloved.
One day, leaving the pleasurable valley of letters,
your hands, fragrant with toil,
came close to me
like the moon above the bullock-carts
to discuss the complexities of politics.
Then one morning when the sun rose
your white smile
turned red all over.
You said:
'Think of me as a flame.'
I shall never lose heart
even if the darkness thickens.
Your smiles
my words
have become the light
of my soul.
I remember the day
when you danced
upon my shoulders.
Even today I feel
there's a gun upon my shoulders.
To my intoxicated eyes
all the trees look like
warriors on horsebacks
their heads camouflaged with leaves.

No, I'm not sad.
Burma and France are astir.
Slogans echo in the enemy camp.
The land of India speaks out.
Only one voice is heard from the jungles:
Forget love. Come and see
how the enemy goes up in flames.

The Colour of the Evening

It's the same old evening again...

Footpaths lead towards habitations.
A lake walks out of an office
having lost its job,
another is quenching its thirst.
The city moves towards the villages.
Someone walks away having lost all his earnings.
Another wipes with the edge of his dhoti
the blood from the whiplashed backs of his emaciated cattle.

It's the same old evening again ...

Once again the winnowers walk away
from an alien land.
A long train of people is on the move
carrying loads of insults
casting long shadows
children riding donkeys
fathers holding their dogs
mothers carrying cauldrons on their backs
with their babies asleep inside.
A long train of people is on the move
carrying on their shoulders the poles for their huts...

Who are these hunger-driven Aryans?
Whose land in Bharat
are they now planning to grab?

The young love dogs.
How can they indulge in the pastime
reserved for the palaces?
Driven by hunger, they are moving out
vacating once again someone's land.
A long train of people is on the move.

They don't know
how many are tied to a post
and burnt everyday.
They who cannot even quit
their habitations.

The shadows cast by trees
are trying to hold down
the feet of mournful cattle
and of sad-faced loved ones.
A long train of people is on the move.
A long train of people is on the move.

Everywhere
the brave peasants are on the move
on their way to the forest
with the weight of spears on their shoulders.
Their love for the fields murdered
a flame has lit up from the huts.
A long train of people is on the move.

The Unemployed

You have learnt the art
of hiding the worn-out edges of your shirt sleeves
of walking with ease in battered shoes
of wagging your tongue to say sweet things
of smiling while hiding corpses under your eyelids ...

But your dress and skin are transparent like glass.
I can see blood coursing through your body
because we have met so often
in third class compartments
at the tea stalls and junk shops.
I too have gathered together my papers
the babu at the employment exchange
flung through the barred window.

The Distance

This isn't the distance between Earth and Mars
that rockets can measure
nor the distance
between Delhi and Moscow or Washington
that you measure everyday
This distance
between you and us
is such
as only arrows can measure

Nadeen[3]

I have fallen in love
with this flower smelling of the earth,
with the colour of this trowel.
The handle's smoothness
that has come through a repeated clasp of the hand
is more beautiful than any work of art.
The veinous hand that remained
the trowel's friend through the rainy season
is the furrowed brow of a warrior.
And this warm stale smell
rising from the shrivelling flowers!
I feel like bursting into song
for these fading colours.
Even though the sun has shone for them
the great rains have washed,
and the winds have kissed their faces,
what if the trowel worked against the sun,
insulted the winds,
rebuked the soft heart of the rain!
I may be a wheat stalk
or this flower
that grows as a weed
I would love the sharp sweep of the trowel;
and all the pain within these flowers,
expressing which this heartless trowel too
is crying with these weeping colours.
Don't let its tears fall to the Earth
The girl's back will break with their weight.

My Country

My country has yet another name.
I have yet another kinship:
where there's even one street
half hungry
half asleep,
where drudgery
counts the stars
to comfort its aching limbs,
wherever it is
away from my homeland
it is my own country, my own brotherhood.
Whenever I pluck the strings of my sitar
to play a tune for this fraternity,
hordes flock towards me from across the seas.
But who's there to welcome them?
Who are they that shed rivers of blood
across these boundaries every year?
My country has yet another name.
I have yet another kinship.

Sanskriti

What are you?
Why have you covered your face?
Why do you walk, so disguised?
Why are you hiding your claws?
But who are you?
Just watch that man
who day and night
pulls a heavy chariot.
His ears are sealed with Manu's molten lead.
His body is striped with
the rulers' whiplashes —
he will surely recognize you.
When, sometimes at night,
he lets out sighs
as big as the skies
the stars lose some of their brightness.
He says: 'This earth is my first love.'
and casually adds: 'It is I
who has bejewelled the sky with these stars.'
He has wandered through Jesus lands
He has roamed through Gautam lands
His ears are sealed with Manu's molten lead.

The Words

The words have been said
long before us
and long after us
You may, if you can,
cut off our tongues
but the words have been said

Goodbye

Goodbye, O the setting sun,
you must come again.
I shall bow my head
but I shall not perform the hypocritical act
of offering water to you:
I shall take up arms.
All right, don't come.
People will take up arms.
You may hide even the moon
but I shall take up arms.
Don't you know?
Mankind too is the fire of the same sun
whose song lights up many lamps like you.
Namaskar
Goodbye
O the setting sun!

Footprints

Can't you see!
Each tree is dancing
the dust on the pathways breathing
the water from the wells spilling out
the water in the canal raging
The peasants are on the move
and the pathways are stamped
with the warriors' footprints
The moon is no longer on the wane

The Dance

When the labourer's wife
bakes her heart on a *tawa*
the moon smiles through the *shisham* tree.
Her husband drums an empty bowl
to humour their younger son.
The elder one dances, and
sets jingling the tiny bells girding his waist.
Then, it seems
neither the song
nor the dance
can ever end.

On Diwali Night

The reeds must be swaying in the wind.
The flowing waters
must be waiting
to kiss someone's eyes,
eyes that become wet for nothing.
At the river bank in the evening
someone's eyes must be fixed
on the quay.
O winds, carry my greetings
and say:
'Don't feel heartbroken
like this for someone today.'

Faith

Just as there's everything on earth:
wheat, sweetness, iron and dynamite
there's everything in people:
waves, floods, storms
pride, dignity, and revolution.
Yesterday a comrade, a Christ look-alike
raising storms through slogans
was chained.
The history
of the *sacred cauldrons, hot plates* and *saws*[4]
was repeated.
Even after all his limbs were broken
his Lenin-like heart remained unshaken.
Hot blood boiled for revenge.
Countless warriors
carrying innumerable rounds of ammunition
marched through the mango groves
unmindful of their heads.
The bodies of those who always drank others' blood
were stuffed with dynamite.
The hands that had hanged the Christ-like comrade
were shot through.
The slogans that go up in Kerala, Bengal, Assam, Nagaland
came from *Chamkaur*[5]
so all may understand
that everything resides in people:
waves, floods, storms,
pride, dignity, and revolution.

Love's Self-Murder

I had wished to write my name
on the face of the moon
together with yours
and share my joy
with every speck.
That's what I was
enraptured in my love.
Why couldn't I unravel
the mystery of *your* love?
You never met me again
not even once.
Striving with ascetic determination
I wandered through all the forests
swam across all the oceans
groped through all the skies
but I could find nothing in you
that was you.
Truth dawned on dim-witted me
when I moved in the marketplace:
my name was tacked with yours
as someone should place
a mucky rag upon a silken dress.
I'm the spirit of a father
trampled upon in the fields.
The heart of a mother
robed in tatters.
I wonder how you withstood
this talk of the town.

You must have spent sleepless nights
and the chatter of dry leaves
driven by wind
must have sounded
like people sniggering at you.
The eyes that once flooded with tears
if they missed me
would now panic
should they fall upon my face.
If my face burns your eyes like cinders
I won't wait for you.
If it demeans you among people
I won't light any lamps.
I won't wait for you.

Caste

O you of another caste
in love with me
our families don't even burn their dead
on the same ground

Not Reflected in Your Mirrors

We don't accept anything
given in charity.
Neither heaven
nor the rule of a righteous king
nor any socialism.
Please tell us
who you are
to do anything for us?
You fear for our blood
being spilled!
People shall kick
the pots in which
you plan to save our blood.
We refuse to see ourselves
reflected in your mirrors:
neither any ray of hope
nor any kind of dream
through someone's charity
do we accept.

A Thought

Those moments were dry
when I mistook your rich moist hair
for salvation

The Outcasts

Cleaning up mangers
gathering cow-dung
or wheat spikes:
they work very hard
these gentle outcast daughters.
Spiky straw, hot plates,
sharp-edged vegetable cutters,
needles –
as if all these had been trained
to hurt their hands and feet.
This iron basin,
resembling the helmet
on her soldier husband's head,
that one of them always carries on her head
makes her look like a warrior.
I have seen her dance.
I have seen her sing.
Ouf! When they cry
it seems colourful walls were soaking.
Who can watch this?

The Song of Radium

The power of darkness is such
that traversing through long nights
lamps lose their breath and die
but radium never,
never ever
stops singing its song,
and drives away despair from the doorsteps.
Darkness intensifies its colour
filling every speck with its blackness
casting 'Dil' into the boiling cauldron of anger.
The song of radium overflows with compassion
independent of any sun.
Radium never stops singing
and drives away despair from the doorsteps.

A Song

The morning of a blessed life
shall surely dawn one day.
You may burn us in your golden lamps
leaving only darkness for us.
Tomorrow we shall stand upon
the debris of flattened mansions.
Look at the rising storm.
Go and face it head on.
Your stock of words
directed from majestic heights
shall not last long.
Crowns will rot in animal dung,
flowers from your thrones fade away.
The morning of a blessed life
shall surely dawn one day.

Kangla Teli

1

When Kangla Teli[6] was young
Old Bhoj[7] went far and wide
in search of prey.
By a row of huts one day
his caravan of chariots passed.
The vizier from a distance saw:
'Maharaj! See that moon-faced maiden,
the one carrying a pitcher,
a delicate marble statue.'
As Bhoj turned and looked
the marble shape trembled in fear.
Turning red, it covered its face.
The caravan was halted.
Bhoj and his vizier stepped out.
One by one the villagers made their obeisance.
The village elders were summoned.
Rehmatan's father came and said:
'Maharaj, my daughter's wedded
to Peerudit Teli's son Kangla.'
The vizier retorted:
'Old fogey, dare you pit Kangla against Raja Bhoj!'
The mother stood reclining against the door,
Rehmatan drenched in tears.
Crying in their hearts
the women led her to the chariot.

2

Peerudit, Teli of another village,
often skirmished with rajas.
His chums honoured him.
Mischief-makers feared bold Peeru.
His son Kangla, brave as a lion,
in clashes between villages
would be at the forefront,
carrying his stick on his shoulder.
Village girls were dearer than his own sisters,
mothers dearer than his own mother.
Peeru would barter oil
for an equal measure of ghee.
Once Kangla thrashed
the court hooligans.
Yet behind his back
people said:
'Kangla's no match for Raja Bhoj'

3

Dead drunk, Raja Bhoj
went to his bedchamber upstairs.
From a distance Rehmatan saw him
stagger into the curtains and fall.
Then he neither moved nor spoke.
From the window Rehmatan saw
glowworms glimmering in the darkness,
stars strung above the wilderness
extending for miles around.
Far away a lamp glowed
as if lit by her mother.
It seemed Kangla waited down below
with a band of armed youth
who had formed his marriage party.
Invoking the vast wilderness as mother
Rehmatan jumped down from above.

4

The night ended.
Raja Bhoj, now sober,
rose from the marble floor
and saw the empty bed.
Through their soft light, the diamonds said:
'Rehmatan couldn't be held captive.'

5

The news reached Peeru's ears:
Rehmatan has been abducted by Bhojpal.
Yet another, like his own sister,
had been robbed of her honour.
The moment he heard this
Peerudit took his last breath.

6

Kangla, who was far away,
heard only this:
Bhoj had seduced Rehmatan
and burnt her alive the next day.
He neither spoke nor laughed.
When he reached his village
people had already buried
Peeru's body under loads of earth.
His shoulders weighed down by grief,
Kangla staggered along walls.

7

He rode to the doors of Peetu *bhangi*[8]
and tied his white horse to a stake.
A cloth wrapped round his head,
his beard covered in dust,
Peetu embraced and kissed Kangla.
'Friend, our honour binds us.

We exchanged our turbans long ago.
Turban brothers are we five.
It's sinful to now eat or drink.
My hatchet lying in the manger
stared at me the whole night.
My mare keeps kicking the walls
in anguish for your pain, brother Kangla.
My chest is clogged with lava.
Last night my enemies said:
Peetu *bhangi's* no match for Raja Bhoj.'

8

One cold evening
Raja Bhoj and his vizier
rambled far out from the palace.
Breathless horses and mares
suddenly drove into the palace.
First the two guards were slain.
Young men their faces masked
hatchets and spears in hands
galloped through the palace, searching.
Letting the reins go
they dismounted,
broke the doors open with hatchets.
Peetu searched each nook and corner.
Soon after, flames rose,
the bedecked ceilings collapsed.
Anyone who resisted
was cast into the fire.
As morning came, rumours were rife.
Old men remembered Kangla.
Here and there weary old men
spoke in failing voices: 'You fools,
Kangla's no match for Raja Bhoj.'

9

Royal soldiers carrying spears and shields
patrol the villages, riding their horses.
Thirsty and hungry
they pass by quickly, fearing.
All the young seem like Kangla.
Sticks in the hands of bent old men
look like hatchets.
They who see their faces
in the morning, wonder:
would they get to eat that day?
Women throw curses at them..

10

One day, Kangla and some others
passed by a fair on a pond's edge.
Parading their buffaloes, sheep and mares
grass-cutters, herders, and tillers
came and spoke sweetly to Kangla.
The tillers and herders sang.
Beeru *Mir*[9] played the *dhadh*[10].
With the day gone the fair dispersed.
All readied their mares and horses.
Beeru *Mir* said, with folded hands:
'We shall also go with our friends,
we may or may not meet again.'

11

A caravan stopped by the riverside
in the soft morning sunshine.
Thirteen warriors from three chariots alighted
armed with swords and arrows.
They took the footpath along the river
walking in line.
Raja Bhoj moved among them

a bow drawn along his shoulders.
The warriors spread out far and near
in search of prey.
While Bhojpal was looking for deer
among a thick grove of trees,
a *lion* challenged him from rear.
The moment Bhojpal turned
his crown was tossed into bushes.
Young men jumped from trees
and attacked each and every one.
Kangla came close to Bhojpal
and unmasked his face.
He didn't open his eyes again...
Later, from the dry woodland
flames rose like lava.
The whole caravan to flames consigning
Kangla wept bitterly, fearing
Rehmatan too might have perished.
One by one, Kangla searched
all the chariots.
Peetu came there too,
riding his mare and screaming:
'The flames are all around us.
O brave Kangla you have done wrong.
How shall we show our faces?
No man, no horse survives.'

12

From village to village, city to city
rumours spread faster than wind.
Some said Bhoj was killed by a lion
when he went hunting.
Some said Kangla had buried Bhoj
deep under the earth.
Some said in failing voices:
'Kangla's no match for Raja Bhoj.'

The Red East

The big ball of the sun
rises from the red red east
enveloping within a red haze
the hamlets just waking up,
the begrimed house tops
the shanty doors.
Habitations where, wrapped in red dust,
hungry, tender-bodied girls are seen
heaving heavy baskets.
Habitations where bare-footed mothers
walk away for the day's labour.
Habitations where the weaver
plying his loom the whole night
collapses into sleep at dawn
as if a heavy wheel in a mill
should suddenly break down,
leaving his children crying for the morning meal.
Habitations where
the whole day long
to ease the pain
of hunger
of deprivation
the neighbourhood women
fight, wrestle
pull at each other's hair
shower abuses
hurl brickbats.
Habitations where any talk of sharing

is greeted with a garland of shoes.
Habitations from where
eyes filled with monsoon tears walk
towards fields
towards mills
towards mines.
Habitations where
old men's heads and beards tremble
in the clatter of hoes and hammers.
Habitations where blacksmiths
keep awake the whole night
their lives burning out with their lamps.
Habitations where peasants
feed on humiliation
having to sell off even the whey.
If they come out
their mortgaged fields
break their hearts,
if they sit at home
they fear the beam may collapse
on their heads.
The landowner drives past
the peasant scratching his dishevelled head
singeing the skies
blotting out the sun with smoke.
Habitations where
the wives of peasants
swoon fear-stricken.

The red ball of the sun
becomes bigger
rises higher up.
Tangled in its rays
playing like a gramophone record
red words
red light

reach the waters
carrying this song:
'The east wind
is threatening the west today.'
Another song:
'Enemies of people
the wealthy
the rulers
the landowners:
all are paper tigers.'
And another song:
'Get to the root of evil.'

The red ball of the sun
becomes bigger
goes up still higher
sending this message:
'O people who gather straw
gather ideas.'
And this message:
'O people awake in shanties
the revolution is born in jhuggis.
O people awake in the fields
the revolution grows in fields.
O people rotting along the drains
the revolution flows from
the barrel of a gun.'

The sun's red ball
becomes bigger
and rises still higher.
O proud dollars
O foolish roubles
the sun cannot be hidden.
The sun's red ball becomes bigger
rises still higher.

The Prison Wall

Wherever a piece of plaster
peels off the prison walls
we see imprinted
the image of the sickle and hammer.
I too have come here
with a new determination:
to add to the sickle and hammer, a spanner
for tightening the nuts and bolts,
for we're too slow
and darkness moves like a rocket.

Lepers

Conscience and vision have rotted.
The body is leprosy-stricken.
Principles, art, literature,
and a mountain heap of books
on which the leprous hands of scholars ply
lie in the open
ruffled by the wind.
The picture frames of idealism
have been defaced and cast upon garbage heaps.
Having beautified their homes
the lovers of Mona Lisa
threaten with atom bombs
but bombs have already exploded.
Conscience and vision have rotted.

FROM **BAHUT SAAREY SURAJ/SO MANY SUNS**

(1982)

Insurgence

When
that dark-complexioned woman
overflowing with joy
says: 'I'm a bastard out and out'
she hurls so many things,
like me,
into the fire under the coal tar drum:
images
books
the roof under her feet
and
brickbats brickbats brickbats

After the Day's Toil

After the day's toil
they tie in a corner of their dress
the day's wage for their child's labour
plead for two chapattis
beg and beseech
talk about the wife's illness
laugh heartily
relapse into dead silence
and walk away

Punjab

It's Punjab everywhere:
all around
villages surrounded by trees.
The appearance hardly distinguishable
veiled under a bundle of grass
a dirty towel
an unkempt beard
a shirt black with sweat and dust
bare legs
cracked heels.
Whether in Bengal
or in Kerala
the herdsmen, driving their cattle
through a haze of dust
look like Punjabis.
The *peepul* trees
the date palms
along the footpaths
the clouds:
it's *Machchiwada*[11] all around.

Tribal Women

The tribal women come,
they pull and pluck fruits.
They have their babies in their laps.
They say:
We were queens.
We married off our servants
among the forest folk.
These bounties
were given away by our men.

All is Poetry

A manure-starved crop
is poetry
An over-manured rotting field too
is poetry
The mill is poetry
The tyrant's dagger
is poetry
His defeat too
is poetry
The mills
running like chariot wheels
heavier than train wheels
are poetry
The ice-vendor Jattoo's body
burns with fever
The burning forest too
is poetry
There's poetry in my father's laughter
Wherever he walks he wears himself out
laughing, whatever he may laugh at
The ploughshare pointing upwards
and the seeder tube
are poetry
The mill is poetry
Children sucking ice-candies in fairs
are poetry
Wrestlers who give up wrestling
having lost their vigour

are poetry
The mill is poetry
Kerala is poetry
Today Bengal is pure poetry
There are a hundred poems inside a stone
a hundred poems inside steel
a hundred poems inside me
The mill is poetry
People hauling stones
beating drums
talking of nothings
are poetry
The mill is poetry
In the evening
the donkey drovers
the snake charmers
the winnowers
all are poetry
The mill is poetry
The tyrant's dagger
is poetry
The dagger on the tyrant's neck
is poetry
The mill is poetry

The wave

Shall this wave subside?
Now the ships can't even cast anchor
The waters have become still deeper
Birds flap their wings
to pull the rising waves upwards
Shall this wave longing to defeat death
subside?

A Letter

The bricks on the ruined wall across,
O my soldier,
take on many loving shapes.
Your dead father's creditors,
O my soldier,
knock at the door every day.
The lamp remains lit
all night,
O my soldier.
The crematoriums are ablaze
and the nights are still
like vultures at rest,
O my soldier.
If I sleep
they scream
all night,
O my soldier.

To Friends in a Military Vehicle

O friends sitting in the military vehicle
your faces, your uniforms tell
you have been newly recruited
and are being driven far away.
You can read a quizzical look on my face.
Yes, I have something to say to you:
O friends, making your way through crowds,
your eyes tell me
even today your helpless fathers
must be toiling somewhere for bread
or your mothers walking, like frightened animals,
to work as daily wagers.
And if you are farmers, you are going away
having sold out your meagre lands.
Or the policeman might have kicked once again
your brother's basket of wares.
You're going away to protect the mills? Goodbye!
Mills where fat is squeezed out of humans
where a worker's skin is turned into hide.
Will you be able to go on long marches
your head held high like *shisham* trees?
Trees from where mothers picking dry twigs
are browbeaten to climb down?
You're going for the sake of palaces? Goodbye!
The palaces where during a war
the inventory of gains dances at night.
You're going to defend the borders? Goodbye!
Such disputes are the lifeblood of politics.

You're going to a place, my friends,
without knowing,
where the bayonets are pointed, out of fear,
at hungry crowds;
where the earth's motion is arrested
by burning down hamlets;
where *Naxalites* are parading
holding flaming torches in their hands;
where there are no jungles with tall trees
and tiny tea-leaves have armed themselves.
You are going to a place
you don't know...

Teeth Sharper than Ploughshares

We're Jats.
We're tired.
We can't fight.
The land has slipped away from under our feet.

Make us touch the land.
We're Jats.
We're never tired.
We shall fight.

O *Banda*[12]
you're from Jammu,
the Guru had bidden you
not to marry.
Just tell us,
O the Lion of Punjab,
where shall we strike:
at your mother-in-law's bed
or at the white man?[13]
Bhupa Avatar[14] once again
overshadowed everyone like a cloud
naming his daughters *Jagiro.*[15]
Today it's '47.
We shall kill the babies in their wombs.
Then all the land shall be ours.

I'm a Jat.
All the Jat votes are mine,

cinemas, the opium stalls, all are mine.
Jats have electricity, machines.
Our garages, our godowns are stacked with fertilizers.
They aren't Jats
whose teeth are sharper than ploughshares.

Night

O my dear, I'm enslaved by debt.
They force me to reap the paddy.
You and I
and our children
live on your labour.
O my dear, draped in a single sheet,
how they force you to reap the paddy!
I smoked away the bidi
saved for the next day
and the whole day passed
craving for one.
O my life, I'm enslaved by debt.
In my dream
my thatched roof was blown off,
empty pots went flying.
They force me to reap the paddy.
A dream overshadowed your face.
You combed the fireplace;
there was no fire.
How they force you to reap the paddy!
I was sold
like all the rest.
Children are carried in laps and sold.
My eyes are drowsy with sleep.
O my dear, I'm enslaved by debt.

The Women of Kudeli Village

The women of Kudeli, wearing black,
pass through gardens green
to labour in the fields.
They know Ravana's people wore black
even then they wear black.
They know the demons wore black
even then they wear black.
They know the thieves wear black
even then they wear black.
When in the wet season
the gardens burst into green
black shines through them.
They know Kudeli is the name of a she-serpent
the most venmous she-serpent
even then their village is named Kudeli.
And they wear black.
They know...

The Innocents

Near naked innocent girls
picking berries
gathering leaves of milkweed
broken pieces of pottery
making mud chapattis
counting the dresses for their doll
dresses as old and ragged as their own
wrapping berries in milkweed leaves
all to be displayed as dowry for their doll

Picking berries
the girls walk away for the day's labour

The parents
append their sighs
to the mud chapattis
and the berries,
touch their daughters' heads in blessing
Happiness rises out of the smell
of old and cheap clothes
of cheap soap and face cream:
nothing better than this ever comes their way

The well-being of their offspring
is scorched by constant worries and headaches
The mother drains out her life blood eating dry bread
Children learn to walk
pull her hair

ask for money
The mother hands out a few berries
out of her pocket
then a slap on the face
hands out a few berries
out of a vessel
then a slap on the face
Wipes out the last traces of salt
from the vessel
as she sings
of her young brother-in-law's love

Innocent mothers tease each other
while picking berries

And those whose god
has walked away on the footpath to death
pass their youth like stones
Struggling on life's muddy ways
they neither pick berries
nor tease anyone

If this story were ever told
to the inhabitants of another star
they would turn into stone
and never wake up
Were the animals to sense this
they would flee to the jungles
shrieking, in fright of mankind

Nammah

We were very young then.
The women had driven us out
from the swarm of *giddha*[16] dancers.
Then Nammah's woman had danced
stripping herself.
She could dance
holding a cot between her teeth
or carrying a pitcher full of water.
Even today at marriages
she sings a song in a mellow sing-song voice
in which a young man declares:
'O *Vahiguru,*[17] *I refuse to be your Sikh.*'
When the crops ripen
she becomes youthful again.
As the stars come out
she joins the farm labourers
carrying food and scythes.
Nammah has seen much in life.
His son could not stand even a few blows
of unemployment
and went mad
kicking up a rumpus about his grandfather's hookah.
When Nammah was boiling sugarcane juice
he came and said:
'Sometimes you became my father
and sometimes I.
These are games
the cycle of birth and rebirth plays.'

Then adding:
'Look, I'm going to jump into the boiling cauldron.'
Horrified, the people around dragged him away.
Nammah kept dipping the charred poker
into the boiling cauldron
to stir the thickening cane syrup.

During a war
during elections
during festivals
he walked home
at the same even pace.

On moonlit nights
during the rainy season
his plough must have plied
in every field.

His trowel
his feet
his sweat
on each speck of the soil.

Short-sighted
carrying his pale-faced father's stick
herding others' cattle
people have called Nammah a godly man
since the days he was young.
At the time of his marriage
he had asked his mother
for two black *tehmats*[18] and
a pair of embroidered shoes.

Sometimes at a marriage
or on a festive occasion
he dances

in the company of the young
or his equals in age.

He gets dead drunk
shuts his eyes and clicks his fingers.
Horrified, his companions make him sit
and hand him a large stiff drink.

A Song

Give us a wide world
wider than the blue skies
one family one piano
one home one hearth
Let storms raze
the church and the mosque
Let a hurricane blow away the temple
Let people sing of hard work
Forget *Heer-Ranjha*[19] and *Dulla-Bhatti*[20]

Let no one's bread be snatched
Let no one be stripped off his clothing
Let's listen to our hearts
Let's celebrate and have fun

Father, in Your Fields

O father, sometimes
I break into a dance
in your fields,
like the passing breeze,
forgetting
the fields don't belong to us.
Just to please my heart!
We have lost the case
for want of money.
The shoes have worn out
the nails in the sole are showing.
Tractors will dance one day,
father, in your fields.

A Game

On moonlit evenings
under the shadows of the *peepal* tree
or in the lanes
they would form a train
holding the backs of each others' shirts.
They moved around screaming:
'Bahun bahun hulla... bahun bahun hulla
Inqila... Jindaba...Inqila... Jindaba'
till the moonset
or till they heard their parents call
and the sound of doors being shut,
forgetting
they were far more naked than Gandhi.
One day they saw
the game they played
was being played by a very *old man*[21]
whom dozens of policemen
had hauled off in a jeep.
They were frightened.
For days
the pleasant shade under the *peepal* tree
kept waiting.
The *koel*
whose call they used to imitate
flew far away
towards the horizon
feeling sad.

Prisoners' Headman

He was prisoners' headman in the jail...
That day he was strolling under the *neem* tree
naked, in his loincloth.
He came and stopped in front of my mill
spread his arms wide
trotted like a horse
and shouted:
'Our fields...our fields',
then walked away.
He was the son of a tenant farmer.
He had speared to death
the son of the landlord
who was the same age.

Wailing Ruins

(for Bodhi, the forest-dweller)[22]

For centuries
the brave have been wailing among ruins
just as a mother would cry over her son's grave.
Here the crickets sing
snakes dance
termites haul mud up their mounds
reeds overgrow
light is dead and darkness rules
but
even in death the brave travel across centuries.
Once these ruins were our homes
we had mothers
we had brothers
we had sisters
our world was free.
But like trees among the termite mounds
we are fearless.
Lions baulk
while passing by.
Sometimes
from the ruins
wails light up
like fire from phosphorous
a flame of hope,
of great hope .

In the Beginning

Nothing was older than the skies,
if there was, it was nothing.
In the beginning was Shiva, or it was Ganga
that flowed out of Shiva's eyes
for centuries
on separation from Parvati
after he was driven out of heaven
for the sin of eating corn.
At the beginning were the Vedas
or the Ramayana
when there was no *Tulsi*[23]
nor anything created by him.
At the beginning were Dravidians
when there were no Aryans
nor the English

When the Forest Burns

After the forest has burnt down
the newly sprouting shoots
the blades of grass
sharp, green or yellow
the soil —
everything becomes fragrant again.
But here
after every fire
rises a stink
in which the soil is helpless.
Shoots sprout and grow in that stink:
the whole forest comes up again.
We remain enslaved.

Proof

Proof is demanded
to make a mockery of truth.
The grass
the straw
the broken pots
the wounds –
all are proof.
If you have a gramophone
then pick up any piece of a broken pot
from these ruins
where we are imprisoned
and play it like a record.
But you won't do that
and we don't have a gramophone.
Prisoners have only dreams
and in dreams
the sun, the moon, the stars, the earth
are all time-honoured records.

Motherland

Love knows no reason
and fragrance has no roots
Truth may or may not have a motive
but a lie is never motiveless
Not for your blue mountains
not for your blue waters
Had they been the colour
of an old mother's pale hair
I would have loved you even then
Your vast treasures
are not for me
Nevertheless
love knows no reason
A lie is never motiveless
The serpents guarding the treasures
sing your praises
They call you a golden sparrow

The Lamp, the Pen and the Notebook

My salutation to this lamp
in which the oil burns
through a thick cotton wick
and whose flame radiates heat and fragrance
that spreads around, far and wide,
touching the feet of Dravidians
who perished fighting against the first Aryan invaders.
An ocean overflows from the pen.
The paper and the notebook
are like the leaves of fragrant trees
that the rebellious wear on their heads
like turban crests
like spearheads.

The Once Powerful

They move from pillar to post
chanting, 'Yes sir, yes sir'.
Sit in dark corners.
They are told
they were born from a god's feet.
The once powerful wander helplessly
waving flies off their eyes,
walk with heads bent down.
They believe
their biceps
their legs
are just tools for drudgery.
Nothing more.
It is hidden from them
they were Dravidian.

Weariness

O this weariness!
This state of inaction!
A thought worms through my brain.
Should someone provoke me:
'Your innocent girl was crushed under a wheel.'
May be then...
If I came to know
my brother had gone mad
I might be shaken a bit.
If someone said:
'Your mother has been disrobed by the police',
this might roll over quietly
like a wheel
without hurting.
The weariness is only in the limbs.
I can see the buffalo's eyeball shining
in the earthen-lamp's light.
Sweeping its droppings everyday
I believe I'm a Shakespeare
whose innumerable mornings and evenings
are spent inhaling dung.
The strength of my arms
neither ebbs nor flows.
My heart yearns to cause an upheaval:
to lift this mountain
and with one push of the shovel
sweep these buildings off the roads.
Dogs bark:

'My home! My home!'
The landlord:
'My village! My kingdom!'
The leader:
'My country! My country!'
People:
'Our fate! Our fate!'
What should I say?
This weariness!
This state of inaction!
My brother? My friend? My daughter? My mother? My country?
Nothing is mine.
My heart yearns to cause an upheaval.

Prostitutes[24]

Friends!
You may despise me as much as you like.
These prostitutes
are my mothers, sisters and daughters
and yours too
and they are mothers, sisters and daughters
of the cow-worshipping India
and they are mothers, sisters and daughters
of Bharat, the worshipper of non-violence and the Buddha
and they are mothers, sisters and daughters
of the big capitalists.
If not
then they are mothers, sisters and daughters
of the imminent revolution.

A Wonder

Woman is a wonder of this world
(all else is much less)
that has given us life's elixir since the beginning
filling new colours in this picture ever since.
Eyes haven't tired looking at her for ages
desire becoming more intense.
People say the earth rests on a bull's horns.
I disagree.
I am firm
that woman carries the earth upon her hands.
That's why the earth smells of a woman's body.
That's why the crops wave like women's scarves.
That's why the waters are so cool and clear.
That's why leaves rustle on moonlit nights
like silver-sequined *dupattas*.
That's why flowers have the innocence of her lips,
butterflies the intoxication of her eyes.
The earth and woman share the same pain.
Those who toil are hungry.
The tyrannized have tears in their eyes.
Woman has tears in her eyes.
That's why the seas are brackish.
Today she loves her pride.
Today she is closer to the stars.
Woman is a wonder of this world.

Culture High and Low

Yes, the snakes are *Satyugi*[25] even today
lying under the Himalayas
deep in the sands of dark oceans.
Yes, there was a time when the skies
seemed like an image of the human heart.
Lovers were true to their word,
deeply in love.
The *Satyugis* sleeping by the milky lakes
were free
like the moonlight across the skies.
Human beings as yet
were not weighed against cowries
and were simple, white and tall.
Human beings painted snake images upon trees
and said:
'No one is freer than snakes.
They live as they will.
No speech is truer than theirs.
Snakes can never be bitten.'
Then one day the self-willing skies
became dead.
People who said,
'No one is freer than snakes'
were imprisoned on the banks of ponds.
Human beings enslaved human beings.
Silenced to speak of snakes
People could not even say:
'No one is a greater slave than us.'

They then painted snake images on doors.
Sang of them with the beat of drums.
Drew snake lines
on pots and pans, on their arms.
And then a king saw
that snakes still lived in people's minds
that no poison was stronger than of the snakes
and no earthquake stronger than people,
who might rise in revolt.
Then he chased and hunted and killed the snakes,
effaced them from people's speech
from their arms and walls.
Snakes that lie deep under the Himalayas
that had troubled the hearts of the black tyrants
and still do.
Snakes can never be nose-stringed.
Snakes can never be worn round necks.
Snakes can't be hung on heads.
Even today that imprisoned snake culture,
drinking from ponds, says:
'Don't drive out our ancestors from our hearts.
Even though we're enslaved
we still uphold the snake culture.
Snakes can never be nose-stringed.
Snakes can't be wrapped around heads.
Snakes can't be cast in copper.
Snakes can never be made from gold.'
The *Satyugis* that sleep by milky lakes
can't sleep beside silver heaps.
Snakes never sit on treasures.
There you find only images of nose-stringed snakes
or of dacoits or priests.
Even today the elders
sing the forgotten songs
evoke their snake ancestors
before they put the first morsel in their mouths.

They never kill a snake.
The snakes never beg
neither for food nor for life.
Snakes are great warriors.
They never utter falsehoods,
are never frightened or shaken.
No one can ride the snakes.
Snakes never assume human shapes.
Even then we are caught in the net of beauty and ugliness
Even then we are breathless.
Even then we paint images of snakes.

FROM **SATTHAR /A SHEAF**

(1997)

The Bull

He kicked and raged
before he was gelded
shook everything
and brought the mosque down

Now he doesn't even look back
at the world gone by
and floats in the air
like the fluffy milkweed seeds

Before , when he bellowed
he would dig the earth
with his horns
Now the itch is gone

It makes no difference to him
whether to bellow or stay quiet
or lower his neck under the yoke
at one call

Under the Heels of Counter-revolution

It remained only a dream:
to teach a lesson
to these wicked gentlemen
to make them rub their noses on the ground
to make them pay for their sins.
But it was we
who were crushed under the heels
of a counter-revolution
To suffer humiliations seemed
our only destiny

The Hapless Public

On his return from banishment
Rama asked the people:
How was it?
They said:
The scales were always tipped
against us.
Rama said: Was it so?
It's the same
even today.

A Poem that is not Revolutionary

I wish to write a poem
that is not revolutionary
so I can find a friend
I wish to pare my ideas
of their nails
so I can find a friend
and we two
can become inseparable
But I cannot think of a subject
that is not revolutionary
so I cannot find a friend

Mahatma Ravan

He who was punished in his lifetime
why punish him again and again?
What was that relationship?
That arrow and that heart.
It was no ordinary man's destiny.
He became a mahatma.
Couldn't Ram, the washer man,
who himself was God,
wash off his sins
that were like spume upon sea waves?
What is godhood
without Ravan?
And what is truth
without justice?

The Sparrow Tale

No one is a cat and no one a sparrow,
all are equal.
It has just been imagined that way.
No one is a tiger, and no one a lamb,
if we didn't believe that way.
The royal painter
had made a mistake:
a springing tiger
a fallen goat.
But when everyone imagined that way
the story-tellers behaved like innocent pigeons.
Of course, they weren't
eagles in the sparrow tale.

The Tale of Gods and Demons

A war goes on
between gods and demons.
New weapons, new knowledge.
These call them kafirs,
they liken these to Satan.
No one can tell
who are the gods
and who the demons.
Great warriors
fall unsung.
Every day we only hear, we don't see,
who has overthrown whom.
Fighters multiply
as if the dead have come alive.
Bangles are broken during the night,
crematoriums wake up during the day.
White ants have devoured all promises.
Faith and honour are dead.
Wages are cotton balls for which
people fight among themselves.
No one knows
who's a friend
and who a foe.
They who hold the bows
own lakhs of acres.
Whcn would the powerful
stop tyrannizing the weak?
When would the time come to say:

kirpan is not God?
Neither the earth nor the sky
is visible.
They too are victims
and die everyday.
The sun and the moon angrily watch
the mountains being razed.
We shall find neither buttered bread
nor any friends.
To them this is no matter.
They love bloodbaths.
If they embrace each other
together they will devour all.
For them power comes first
people next.
Curse the weapons
in the hands of the wicked.
They who regard everyone their own
don't demand a theocratic state,
neither do patriots
let religions destroy their motherland.

The Woodworm

As the piece of wood
burns away
the woodworm too
would be pushed into the fire
Even then
it keeps eating
into the wood

O the Golden Ram

O the golden ram
which way will you go?
There's a multitude in the east
a multitude in the west
a multitude in the south.
You will neither move your horns
nor bite anyone.
O the golden ram
which way will you go?
Each face looks innocent
each in saintly disguise
their hands murderous
all waiting
rubbing their palms
like players waiting to catch a ball:
Their claws are deadly trained
to grab your golden fleece.
Whichever way you go
they will bloody their hands.
O the golden ram
Which way will you go?
Whichever way you go
you will face great murderers.
White ones here and blue ones there
but how does that help you?
Those who stand by
won't even cough!
O the golden ram
which way will you go?

To Sant Ram Udasi[26] and Other Poets of My Tradition

Some words cannot die
but only those sung by a revolutionary.
Why shed tears?
Why talk of humiliations?
You're a unique sun
that spreads light all round.
This tower of red light
would light the whole world forever.
Arms broken, pains unbearable
but you neither groaned nor feared.
If we're sad, no one consoles.
Blows and deceptions still await us.
Those who don't sing the song of justice
die the death of donkeys.
But suns do their duty
and spread light everywhere.
An eternal war goes on
between light and darkness.
Where light fails to keep watch
darkness pitches its tent.

Passengers

Passengers
whose luggage
is left behind
look through the window
of the express train
longing to deboard
for a dream-like luggage

Fate of the Queens

One lost her life
Another
tousled hair
bare-footed
gathers dung –
both deprived
of their beds of luxury

The Soldier

You had detailed them
to take a position
against the wind
and stand firm:

Trees fell
lights toppled
an arm fractured
a sword broke
Someone still stands
his body twisted
Another fell
taking much with him

In the shrieking wind
in the intensifying darkness
of the dark nights
they didn't give up
didn't stop smiling
didn't shift their gaze

The Letter

I was shaken
by looking just at the face of the letter
miffed as I already was.
How did the diamond look
before it became Koh-i-Noor?
Was it history
or the artisan's skill
that set its value?
I couldn't summon the courage
to read and know
how momentous was the letter's content.

Wherewithal

When my children
have the wherewithal
I wonder
what all they would produce
O dear!
Gardens
O dear!
Crops
O dear!
They would do wonders
when my children
have the wherewithal

Song of the Comrades

We're true comrades, O folks
We're true comrades...
We're friends with the enemy
We've duped you, O folks
We're comrades...
We can fill the world with words
but cannot stake our lives, O folks
We're comrades...
We won't talk of the revolution
It calls for sacrifice, O folks
We're comrades...
Misled in your innocence
you're hungry and naked, O folks
We're true comrades, O folks
We're comrades...

Two Brothers

The two brothers
went their own ways
yet they were brothers.
Each hated the other
yet they were brothers.
Both knowledge and ignorance
were born in them
and both of them knew
but pretended ignorance.
Yet they were brothers.
They thought well
of learned men,
for at times they did think of their own good.
They fought bitterly
yet they were brothers.
When they were enslaved
they regretted they had forgotten
they were brothers.
Now they openly declare
they are not brothers
and call a snake-like whip
their friend
that rouses them like a friend
and they confront each other
like enemies.

The Reins

Who is holding the reins
and driving you away ...
You didn't get your fodder.
Your hide has been sold,
your bones have been priced.
Your tautened reins
don't let you smell your own muzzle.
You want to smell your congealed blood.
Alas! You could see
how delicious your flesh is.

A Jolt

The turban-loops
became loose
the strong teeth
shook at their roots
eyeballs popped out
and what's more
from many a beard
the dye came off
with just one jolt

Samajvaad

Why establish socialism
if you can't end
individualism
Cook the fish
yet keep it alive

Work

When work remains undone
or untouched
one may assume
death is lurking around
When hands
remain idle
then know
you are about to be overthrown

Without Imagination

To sit up
bereft of imagination
is to be like
eggs on a tray
You have dreams
but they have been boiled
Then it's not possible
to bring forth
anything

Wealth

Drunk on their final victory
those sitting on
a heap of wealth
forgot:
this heap
will open its mouth
like an insectivorous plant
and devour them

The Public

O people, let bats hang over your heads
Anarchists have always spread
only anarchy
and now anarchy is spreading everywhere
You're the robbed
they the robbers
O people, let bats hang over your heads

High Caste

A high caste boy and a low caste girl —
What wisdom, what art!
All concur and say, 'O yes, O yes.'
If that happens they write books. But it is poison
if the boy is low caste and the girl high caste.
Be wise, don't fall in love, if you value life.
Without freedom the heart's emptiness remains empty.
Rama on their lips and a dagger under their armpit.
They conspire to stop lovers from meeting.
The devils don't let us live, forget love.

A Strange Town

Should a poet
only write poems
or should he sometimes write a letter?
But to whom?
It would have to be
to the Revenue Minister:
O Minister sahib, you're new,
this is a complaint against your predecessor.
Large portions of land
that were to be allotted
to Harijans
were allotted by the Minister
in the name of his servants.
And when
the patwaris abducted
four school girls,
one of them jumped into a well
but the other three remained captive
with them.
They approached the Revenue Minister.
The Minister said, 'The issue can be settled.
Transfer in the names of my cattle
the land along the river,
allotted in the names of my servants,
there being no member of my family
without land in their name.'
The issue was settled.
Newspapers were silent,

police stations helpless
people divided.
This is the same Minister
who built a college
at one end of the town
an ITI at the other
to forestall a station being built
and the railway line
cut through his fields.

The Man with Eyes Open

The man with his eyes open sees
that the heavyweight
has let soiled water
from his poultry farm
flow into the fields
of the lightweight.
The water will keep flowing
until he sells off his land cheaply
and goes away.
The man with his eyes open knows
he's taking sides
and is silent.

O Breeze from the Sutlej

We're in love with you, O breeze
We have come to you once again
Rise and see into our hearts
We haven't brought our heads with us
We have come crossing the seven seas
thirsting for your waters
The heart touched by your love
becomes the fire of the sun
It sows the seeds of rebellion
It sings the song of freedom

A Cheap Bargain

I should
buy colour for three paise
a roll of thread for two
put a *tilak* on my forehead
wear a saffron dhoti
paint my face
and sit at the village square
playing Rama or Lakshmana
worshipped by peasants
Join crowds at fairs
and amass wealth
so much so much
as if I possessed the *paras*[27]
Currants and coconuts in plenty
and a distillery
I should
buy colour for three paise
a roll of thread for two

Wake up, My Dear

Wake up, my dear, wake up
You alone have to do all this
You have to load the carts, you have to weigh out the merchandise
You have to dig the grass, you have to water the plants
You have to drive the plough
You have to manage the goats, you have to yoke the cattle
You have to plaster the mud walls, you have to lift the *taslas*[28]
You have to awaken those who seem to have slept forever
You too have gone to sleep, tethering your cattle
Yet everything around you is in turmoil
The war between Kauravas and Pandavas never ends
Duryodhana's torso grows new heads

We are Great Wrestlers

We are great wrestlers
Each morning we gird up our loins
to fight against hunger and nakedness
To make and break plans is our training routine
The tactics we employ are deadly:
We seal our lips when we should speak out
We die of thirst when we should quench it
We vow to continue the fight when we should ask for bread
We bring down great wrestlers
by forcing their necks under our knees
We live like donkeys toiling in the fields
Even then we are great wrestlers
Each morning we gird up our loins...

Relationships

All our four sons and daughters
were married off.
No dowry, no gifts.
Why should we celebrate
the marriages of our children
with the beating of drums?
Who has achieved victory over whom?

They have walked towards the cemetery.
There lie asleep their ancestors.
They are putting a sunshade over their graves.

On the other end the crematorium is active.
The village headman's daughter-in-law
had burnt herself.
Yesterday a corpse was cremated
and the day before too.
Here there are no bonds:
the same old story of enmity
between man and woman
for property and possessions.
But for how long?
They burn the living
just as they burn the dead.

Tea Shop

Early in the morning
the glasses wake up from their cases.
Two and a half dozen glasses.
They drive me mad the whole day.
'No sugar...chillies in tea leaves...the milk you use?'
'You can't run a tea shop.'
Sometimes a lawyer reels out a calculation:
'You can make one thousand cups from ten kilos of milk.'
This awakens memories of the liquor shop
and eyes light up.
'Adjust this against the rent.'
'For this I have already paid.'
'For yesterday, you owed me that much.'
Even then someone pays.
The rich guy's counterfeit coin
looks sweet
even to an untrusting man like me.
The glasses return to their cases,
like pigeons to their pigeonholes.
A few have been pinched by some for their drink.
The liquor shop, the craving drives me mad.
What's this, friends,
if one can't make enough
even for a drink?

This Book

O dear, why did you sell
this book?
Where shall I find its enlightened reader?
The tip of the pen has probed
the spot where the thorn pricked.
The page that rent the heart
is marked with a fold.
This book, many years old,
has added a page to my joy.
Sufi poetry, songs of wisdom
from the late Mughal period,
Bulleh Shah, *Wajid* and *Hashim*,[29]
their pens dipped in blood.
I rescued this book from a pedlar
like someone rescuing a bird from a hunter.
Where shall I find its reader?
I rake my brains to know.
That bird has flown away
from my city.

The Nest

As the *mandir–masjid* issue
boiled up
he began to worry
about his own nest.
Ayodhya was far away
and he was not a priest.
The two-acre piece of land allotted to him
threatened his life every moment.
Owners of the land surrounding his
didn't allow the right of way.
The man from whose land
this piece had been sliced
also hotted up
as if it were the *mandir–masjid* issue.
The poor fellow
racked with fear
secretly at night
harvested his crop
as much as he could
gathered it
and carried it to the market.

The Orchard's Watchman

The watchman is lying flat
with his legs stretched wide.
The wind plays with the treetops
tossing them to and fro.
He has the art
to face storm and rain,
thieves and poachers.
Hunger urges him
to pick a few mangoes
to assuage itself.
But the watchman says:
It's better to suffer.
Hunger like a loyal wife says:
What kind of a watchman are you
to have never eaten mangoes to your fill?
Just then he hears a noise from the pathway
and his stick quickly moves in that direction.
Hunger says: How can you manage on this meagre wage?
The watchman says: This day will pass, very soon.
Guarding against bats is far more difficult
than against crows and parrots.
The orchard will be denuded in one careless night.
The light of the stars has been withheld by clouds.
Those who withhold the wages of a watchman won't be happy ever.

The Oil Mill

The oil mill keeps up its dance,
even those trying to escape are ground.
Here all distinctions disappear,
the man holding the basket does not stop.
Sweet smells rise from those crushed,
oil drips down drop by drop.
Here, you and I disappear,
this mill never stops working.
The workers keep feeding it
in moonlight, in sunshine.
The tick-ticking of the mill
awakens in me a poem:
Pride is ground down, with crackling noise —
the worker enjoys it all.
'Dil' can hear the tinkling of bells,
a lot still remains to be done.

Three Thousand Four Hundred Workers

How do you control
three thousand four hundred workers?
They talk, they make speeches
they throw stones.
But what controls so many
that they don't bring about a revolution?

Workers from the Other State

Workers from another state chant
haee ah... haee ah
as they haul a heavy cable
They sing something in a chorus
to galvanize themselves
A woman wearing a blue shawl passes by
sniggering at them

To the Girl Tending Horses

O you who are tending horses
sing a song for me:
I shall certainly like it.
The one that you sang
while grazing horses
your heart filled with sadness,
when the landlord
had hurt your hand with a pickaxe.
Your mother must have writhed in pain.
How did she stand it?
When shall your brothers wake up?
When shall they grow up?
When shall they tend horses?
When shall they pick up the bow?

A Fistful of Love

A fistful of storms
A fistful of earthquakes
A fistful of wars
A fistful of love

Woman's Fate

Swaddled in old cotton wool
caught among the branches
of a *shisham* tree
a tiny soft hand hangs downwards
as if wanting to grasp the earth.
Dropped out of a kite's claws
this severed limb
looks like the clapper of a bell.
It's not Kabir
found alive on the edge of a pond
or Tagore
the seventeenth offspring of his parents.
From its imposing and sublime look
it appears
it must have been a girl.

A Song

We don't care if we die, we just want to have fun, O friend
This struggle is like a ride on a swing, O friend
Don't talk of astrologers and horoscopes to them
They are going to change the very movement of stars, O friend
Have some faith in these madcaps
Why have you stopped listening to them
They who are in love with poison cups
never give up the path of righteousness
Death plays hide and seek with them
like a beloved with a smile on her face
If the heart is free of all doubts, O Dil
just a sign is more than enough

Extracts from

Ajj Billa Phir Aaya / Billa Came Again Today

(2009)

This Dream

Yes, but this dream was strange.

He is from my mohalla,
keeps long hair.
I have seen him squabbling, sometimes.

I saw him in a dream.

This is a frightening scene
which I should not write about
out of fear.
Otherwise who would
tread the path of justice
and show the way?

He is encircled
by a strange crowd.
He is arguing with them.
Gradually the crowd
grows bigger.
I stand so far
that I can do nothing.
People are wearing new clothes.
Some have caught him
by the arms.
From afar
a cart-load of people
can be seen coming.

Now they have alighted
and come close to him.
They have with them
a broad and sharp black dagger.
One of his arms is severed
with the dagger.
Then one of his shoulders
is cut off.
Then the other.
He is being slaughtered with ease
very quietly.
No howling no crying.
All are watching
satisfied that everything is going
as planned.

I ask someone:
What was he saying?
'Nothing.
He was singing a song.'
A section of the crowd
is celebrating.
Women are sitting around a *tawi*
baking chapattis.
The dough smells of flesh.
I walk towards their households.
I can see flesh in every *thali.*

I feel sad
when I learn
this is his flesh.
I flee from there
and reach a sadhu's abode.
Here there is no flesh.
I have a drink of water.

The dream goes on...

I see many shades of religious leaders
in a bus.
The jam-packed bus
has just one front wheel
which comes off
and I fall off the bus.

The dream doesn't end here.
It goes on and on in my head.
Why did no one protest?
Why was I helpless?
Was this just to hammer home
that I was a slave?
Where does he stand
the man speaking for justice?
They celebrate.
They let the man die
and dance the whole night.

I keep saying a million times
it was only a dream.
I can see the man is still alive.
I can hear him speak
in the same old way.
Even then fear clings to my heart.

I wonder
if it was really me
who in that situation
could do nothing.
A slave's life is strange
like that of a dog's
that snatches away food
from his own brood
with one bark.

The Weaver Bird

When we started going to school
neatly dressed,
these landlords, seeing some of us
wearing trousers, would say:
If they became literate
who would work on our fields?

The weaver bird knits his nest
using reed grass,
leaves of sugarcane
making it safe
for his brood
against rain and storm.
No one has yet matched his skill
in building nests
yet a monkey
tears his nest into shreds
and the bird looks for another branch
where no one can reach.

Another Kind of Terror

One kind of terror
among many is
when all the people
go under the tyrant's protection
and pretend to be happy
camouflaging their slavery
behind their laughter.
They don't feel terrorized.
They become enemies
and refuse to acknowledge.
They don't listen to anyone.

Something Unknown

In my poem
I wish to capture something
something unknown
like shooting an arrow in the dark
If that something can't be captured
the poem is like a plant
that does not bear fruit

My City Samrala

This Green Revolution
has forced people
to pen their cattle indoors.
Forced them to buy fodder
and sell milk.
Debts mount.
The milk of Sutlej is drying up.
Some are grinding *bhang* leaves in their palms.
Some are roaming around like the mad.
Some are renouncing the world.
Many are rushing towards the cities.
The cities can't provide work for all.
My city Samrala,
a name that stands for
a battlefield,
has now become the battleground
for the mafia.
Clay pipes
Powders
Poppy husk
Spirit
Injections[30]
Pills
Cannabis
Swallowing and drinking
many are found lying flat
by the roadside,
in the cremation grounds.

A drug addict
lying dead in an isolated spot
is eaten up
by poultry-farm dogs
with relish.

Billa

He is sociable
He doesn't know
what anger is
Black, bobbed and greasy-haired
clipped beard
broad forehead
tall
smiling
sparkling eyes
not cat-like though
a fast talker
brown-complexioned
pants and shirt
army boots
a *rudraksh* necklace
on a silver string
a locket with the goddess's image
rings on fingers

Exclusion

Almost none from our caste
can be found
in any team
in any film
in any respectable profession.
Roots of this plant of *Manuvad*[31]
lie in *patalalok*[32]
and its head touches the sky.

Manu says:
Don't let them rise
if they do
pull them down quickly.

This ruinous cycle
has gone on since long.
They are undoing all that
the Muslims and English
did for us.

My Characters

The characters
in this long poem of mine
don't know
what has hit them.
The land mafia
has attacked the Constitution
and broken its back.
Corruption has reached
arrogant levels.
They have been driven out of jobs
out of schools.
My characters
these wet crows
don't know what's happening.
Their flights of imagination
are like the flight of a headless chicken.
They want to fulfill their daydreams
and get out of their troubles
through gambling and betting.

Daliticide

Faujis had hoped
their sons would be educated
and commissioned
but here you find addicts
fit to work only as wage labourers
busy grinding *bhang* leaves.
They are not to blame.
They have been pushed into this.
It is Daliticide.
Ill-treatment at school, thrashing,
firing Dalit teachers.
They can't even graze their cattle.
The ponds have been filled up.
The grass lands forcibly cultivated.
They are dying in droves
without anyone killing them.

For Us

For us
trees don’t bear fruit
For us
flowers don’t bloom
For us
spring doesn’t come
For us
revolutions don’t come

Our Fate

The butcher Rai's son came
looking for Billa.
He too is addicted to *injections.*
Sometime ago someone had poisoned
Rai's pigs.
No one cared.
Rai's Diwali was ruined.
One can't make much
by selling chicken meat.
Rai's son is a well-built lad
but he's addicted to cannabis
and *injections.*
This killing of animals
is an old game.
Cattle-rearing is the poor man's livelihood
but they can't do that now.
If they do
they have to scrape grass off the water channels.
Often the calves die in wombs.
The bulls have been burnt alive
by hanging burning tyres round their necks.
The usurpers have crossed all limits.
People uprooted and driven by hunger
become drug addicts.
What's worse
The water pumps are going dry.
People think of fleeing to the cities.
The landlords have free electricity.

Paddy, poplars, fish —
The water table is sinking.
These days decency is in short supply
and so is water.
Has the time come for Ganga to dry up
which, according to Chanakya,
happens at the end of each *Yuga?*

Usurpers

They have usurped power
using our vote.
They are thrashing us
with our own shoes.
The police belong to them
and our own leaders
have joined hands with them
to line their own pockets.

To Jagirdars

This poem addresses
the jagirdars
who have always drunk
people's blood.
Thousands of starving people
had appealed to *Banda Bahadur*
that the jagirdars
were sucking their blood.
In anger *Banda* had rebuked them:
You are in thousands
and they a handful.
Why are you helpless?
Can't *you* suck their blood?
When the jagirdars heard this
they had *Banda* arrested.

The Aboriginal Society

That aboriginal society,
the one Shiva himself had founded.
No one was excluded.
There was no differentiation.
Everyone knew
they were all the progeny of one Father.
Today's society is full of discrimination
filled with hatred,
high and low, this caste and that caste,
you and I.

This Aryan Society

A society based on falsehood
an unjust society
a cruel society
that devised ever newer inflictions
for *adivasis.*
The idlers were worshipped
the artisans called lowly.
Only he who wrote things
acceptable to them
was called a great scholar or a poet.
Finally
Manu wrote *Manusmriti*
by which the shudras'
right to learning was snatched.
The scriptures were tempered with.
The myth —
brahmins from Brahma's mouth
kshatriyas from his arms
vashiyas from his breast
shudras from his feet —
was created.
Those who opposed this
had their tongues cut off.
It is a long history.

This Poem

I have been helpless
in the hands of this poem.
I have been forced to write it like this.
The reins are no longer in my hands.
Rather I have been driven by it.
Perhaps the difference between
poetry and what is not poetry
has been lost.
I have no pride in being a poet
nor have I the desire for greatness.
The shadows are lengthening.
The narrative has dissolved into poetry
and poetry into the narrative.
But even then
if this is disapproved
I would be hurt.
It looks as if a new genre
has taken shape.

This Monster

Finally, how shall we deal
with this monster?
He has devoured everything:
Be they donkeys, or horses, or oxen
or camels.
The carts, the land, the crops
the songs, the shouts, the freedom, sharecropping
the grazing fields, the community lands
government properties, the forests,
the compassionate officers, the community life, the ponds...
How shall we reclaim all these
from his stomach?
His weapons are:
combines, tractors
free electricity
homeless labourers
uprooted from their own states.
He has devoured everything...

Notes

1. Refers to Bhagat Singh, Rajguru and Sukhdev whose bodies, after they were hanged in Lahore (23 March 1931), were cremated and the ashes thrown into the Sutlej near Ferozepur.
2. A small thorny tree with sweet-scented yellow flowers.
3. A weed very commonly found in some parts of Punjab.
4. These refer to the atrocities committed on the Sikhs by the Mughals in the medieval period in Punjab. Bhai Dayala was thrown into a boiling cauldron in 1675; the fifth Guru Arjan Dev (1563–1606) was made to sit on a hot iron plate; and Bhai Mati Das was sawed to death. Bhai Dayala and Bhai Mati Das were disciples of Guru Teg Bahadur (1621–1675), the ninth Sikh Guru.
5. A small town in district Ropar, of great importance for the Sikhs. Here Guru Gobind Singh (1666–1708) had fought a fierce battle against the Mughals in which two of his sons were killed. And in the 1970s this was one of the earliest centres of Naxalite activities in Punjab. Lal Singh Dil was a member of the Naxalite group that had raided the Chamkaur police station in 1969.
6. The caste of oil-pressers.
7. A legendary king who ruled the Malwa region in central India during the eleventh century CE.
8. A derogatory term for the scavenger community, regarded as untouchable among untouchables.
9. Mirs are a caste of traditional singers-cum-humorists among the Muslims in Punjab.
10. An hour-glass shaped double faced small drum, played by tapping with hands to the accompaniment of *sarangi* during singing by a *dhadhi* singer in Punjab.
11. A village in Ludhiana district. Guru Gobind Singh was forced to take shelter here and in the jungle close to this village. It also came into prominence during the Naxalite movement in the 1970s.
12. Banda Singh Bahadur (1670–1716), one of the great Sikh martyrs.

Originally a Rajput, he was converted to Sikh faith by Guru Gobind Singh (1666–1708) in Nanded, Maharashtra, in 1707. He was a great general and administrator who won many battles against the Mughals in Punjab. After establishing his authority in Punjab, Banda Singh Bahadur is said to have abolished the zamindari system. Banda was caught, brought to Delhi, tortured and killed.

13. This reference is to Maharaja Ranjit Singh (1780–1838), the Sikh ruler of Punjab. His mother-in-law, Sada Kaur, once his staunch supporter, fell foul of him in her later life and tried to cross over to the British but was apprehended and kept in protective custody till her death.
14. Bhupinder Singh (1891–1938), Maharaja of Patiala, who, it is said used to abduct beautiful women and keep them in his harem, and later he would allot land (jagirs) to them.
15. A common name among Sikhs for women. In the hope of obtaining jagirs, many people would greedily name their daughters Jagiro.
16. Popular folk dance of Punjab performed by women in a group.
17. A term meaning 'the Wonderful Lord', most often used among Sikhs to refer to God.
18. Also called tamba; a piece of cloth usually worn wrapped around the hips and reaching the ankles.
19. Hero and heroine of one of the most famous romantic and tragic love stories of Punjab.
20. A rebel who led a revolt against the Mughal emperor Akbar in Punjab; he belonged to a Muslim Rajput landowning family.
21. A reference perhaps to the Naxalite leader, Baba Bujha Singh (1888?–1970).
22. A tribal Dil had befriended during his stay in Uttar Pradesh.
23. The sixteenth century Awadhi poet Tulsidas, composer of *Ramcharitmanas*.
24. This poem was published by Amrita Pritam in *Nagmani,* a poetry magazine run by her.
25. Belonging to the Satya Yuga, the golden age in Hindu mythology. The *puranas*, of course, talk of the *nagas* as the inhabitants of the Nagalok, or Patala, the seventh and the lowest region of the underworld. *Vishnu Purana* speaks of a visit by the wandering sage Narada to Patala. Narada describes Patala as more beautiful than Svarga (heaven). Patala is described as filled with splendid jewels, beautiful groves and lakes and lovely daemon maidens.

Sweet fragrance is in the air and is fused with sweet music. Dil seems to be portraying a golden age which, he believes, was the creation of the original inhabitants and rulers of India who were somehow related to the *nagas*. This golden age civilization was destroyed by the Aryans. Dil derived this myth not directly from the *puranas* but most probably from the Punjabi folk cosmology wherein the universe is divided into three realms: Devlok (Sky), Matlok (Earth) and Naglok (Underworld) and the description is similar to the one in the *puranas*. (see Bhatti, H. S. & Michon, Daniel. M, 2004. "Folk Practices in East Punjab", in *Journal of Punjab Studies*, University of California, Vol. 11, No. 2, Fall, p. 140)

26. Sant Ram Udasi (1939–86) was one of the foremost poets of the Naxalite movement in Punjab. His first collection of poems *Lahoo Bhije Bol* (Words Soaked in Blood) was published in 1972. He was a singer with a powerful voice, and during the decade following this collection he was in such great demand that no Kavi Sammelan in Punjab was complete without him.
27. Paras Pathar: A stone believed to turn iron into gold by touching; Philosopher's stone.
28. A large shallow iron bowl for holding plaster for building construction.
29. Bulleh Shah (1680–1757) was a Punjabi Sufi poet. Wajid was a humorous Punjabi poet of the eighteenth century. Hashim Shah (1735–1843) was a Punjabi Sufi poet; best known as the writer of the famous love stories Qissa Sassi–Punnu, Qissa Sohni–Mahiwal and Qissa Shirin–Farhad.
30. Now a Punjabi slang for taking drugs through injections.
31. Way of life as annunciated in *Manusmriti*, especially the caste system and untouchability.
32. The underworld in the Hindu mythology.

Acknowledgements

The number of people to whom I must express my gratitude shows the amount of goodwill and appreciation Dil's poetry enjoys, and the satisfaction it has provided me for having undertaken this very fruitful work.

My understanding of Dil and his poetry has been enriched through my meetings and interactions with persons like Dr. Ronki Ram, Amarjit Chandan, Prem Parkash, Des Raj Kali, Nirupama Dutt, and Dr. Sarabjit Singh, all of whom have known Dil personally and intimately, and talking to them about Dil and his poetry has been of great help. I have also benefitted from my interactions with Dr. Satyapal Sehgal and from his translations of Dil's poetry into Hindi. I acknowledge their debt.

My thanks are also due to Ajay Bhardwaj, the film-maker, who has been kind enough to provide me with a video copy of his documentary, *'Kitte Mil Ve Mahi'* (Where the Twain Shall Meet), which partly features Dil.I am also thankful to another film-maker, Sanjay Kak, who recommended me to a publisher for these translations.

I am also thankful to Prof. (Dr.) Rajesh Kumar Sharma of Punjabi University, Patiala for readily providing me a copy of his article on Dil's poetry published in EPW.

I also express my gratitude to Professor (Dr.) Sukhdev Singh of Panjab University who has been of great help in seeking out Dil's family in Samrala and obtaining their permission to translate Dil's poetry. I cannot forget the courtesy and goodwill shown by him during my meetings with him in Chandigarh. I am grateful to him for permission to include here his article on Lal Sing Dil titled *'Lal Singh Dil's Poetry: A Discourse of Dissent'*.

I am also grateful to all the members of Dil's family for their permission to translate these poems into English. My thanks are also due to my son Rahul who has provided a continuing critique of my understanding of Dil the person and poet, and has always cautioned me against overstepping my limits.

I also thank my daughter Radha for the cover design. I am grateful to Prem Parkash for providing me a copy of one of Dil's letters, which forms part of the cover design.

Thanks are also due to editors, David & Helen Constantine & Sasha Dugdale, of MPT (Modern Poetry in Translation), the Queen's College, Oxford, UK for publishing five poems of Lal Singh Dil (*Nadeen, The Outcasts, The Women of Kudeli Village, The Innocents* and *We Are Great Wrestlers*) translated by me in the *Transitions* issue of MPT (Third Series, Number Eighteen) in 2012 and later including the first two of these poems in the MPT's fiftieth anniversary anthology, *Centres of Cataclysm* (2016), Bloodaxe Books. These poems are reproduced in this collection with their consent.

And finally, I must thank Mr. K.K. Saxena and Rahul Saxena of LG Publishers Distributors who readily agreed to publish this book when I was at a loss for a publisher for some reasons.

T C Ghai